IMAGES OF ASIA
Series Adviser: SYLVIA FRASER-LU

Musical Instruments of South-East Asia

Titles in the series

Musical Instruments of South-East Asia

ERIC TAYLOR

SINGAPORE
OXFORD UNIVERSITY PRESS
OXFORD   NEW YORK

Oxford University Press

Oxford New York Toronto
Delhi Bombay Calcutta Madras Karachi
Petaling Jaya Singapore Hong Kong Tokyo
Nairobi Dar es Salaam Cape Town
Melbourne Auckland
and associated companies in
Berlin Ibadan

Oxford is a trade mark of Oxford University Press

© *Oxford University Press Pte. Ltd. 1989*

First published 1989
Third impression 1991

ISBN 0 19 588894 4

The author has made every effort to trace the copyright
holders of illustrations but, in some instances, without success,
To these, the author and publisher offer their apologies,
trusting that they will accept the will for the deed.

Printed in Singapore by Kim Hup Lee Printing Co. Pte. Ltd.
Published by Oxford University Press Pte. Ltd.,
Unit 221, Ubi Avenue 4, Singapore 1440

Preface

DURING the last century, the outside world has taken an ever-increasing interest in the music of South-East Asia. The turning point came with the Paris World Exhibition of 1889, when the sound of a Javanese gamelan orchestra made a deep and lasting impression upon the young Debussy. Many composers after him—Ravel, Messiaen, and Britten among them—have found inspiration in the characteristic principles of the region's ancient musical traditions and in its distinctive sonorities. The development of air transport has widened the music's audience, with growing numbers of visitors travelling to the region, and with more and more opportunities for native artists to perform abroad.

Exposure to music of remote and unfamiliar cultures at once raises a host of questions. The most difficult are often those relating to the music's inherent principles and to its aesthetic basis: issues which go far beyond the scope of this book, even though they must be at least touched upon since they are at the root of any meaningful discussion of instruments. But formidable problems would still be raised by even the most blinkered concentration on musical instruments as mere physical objects. In South-East Asia, their sheer profusion and their endless variations render generalization perilous, while at the same time making a truly comprehensive account virtually impossible.

Simple answers cannot always be given to apparently straightforward questions. 'What's it called and how do you spell it?', are amongst the most natural and immediate enquiries to make about a strange instrument, yet they raise complex issues, the nature of which demands preliminary mention here. The fact is that an instrument which goes under a certain name in one place may be known by others only a few miles away, while elsewhere the same name may be applied to a different instrument altogether. Moreover, there can be many variations in spelling, many arising out of the difficulties of transliterating non-Roman orthography. Though the trend is towards standardization, there remains a long way to go. The new spelling system introduced by Indonesia and Malaysia in 1972, for example, has not yet entirely superseded earlier usages: thus alternative spellings of the Indonesian city now officially known as Yogyakarta may still be encountered, e.g. Jogyakarta, Jogjakarta, Jogdjakarta, Djodjakarta, Djojakarta, and Djokjakarta.

In the following pages, I have normally used the names and spellings adopted for the principal headings under which instruments are entered in *The New Grove Dictionary of Musical Instruments*, where cross-references are given for many alternatives. Not even that monumental work of reference, however, is exhaustive; nor is it invariably consistent with its parent, *The New Grove Dictionary of Music and Musicians*.

Goring Heath   ERIC TAYLOR
1988

Acknowledgements

I wish to thank the following for their generosity in allowing me to reproduce the photographs shown in brackets: The University of California Press (Plates 10 and 24–from David Morton's *The Traditional Music of Thailand*); the Durham Oriental Music Festival (Plate 5); The Japan Foundation (Plate 22); the authors of *Lordly Shades–Wayang Purwa Indonesia*, privately published in Jakarta in 1984 (Colour Plates 22 and 23); Professor José Maceda (Plate 17); the Tourist Development Corporation of Malaysia (Colour Plate 11); Jabatan Perancang Bandar dan Desa, Perak, Malaysia (Colour Plate 4); Professor Terry E. Miller (Colour Plate 16); the Cultural Center of the Philippines (Colour Plate 8 and Plate 6); the Music and Drama Division of the Fine Arts Department of Thailand (Plates 3 and 4); Thai Airways International (Colour Plate 18); Mr Tom White (Colour Plate 20); and the postal authorities of both Malaysia and Thailand (Colour Plate 6). Photographs which appear by arrangement with the institutions concerned (as acknowledged in the captions) are: Colour Plate 9 (The British Library); and Colour Plates 12 and 13, and Plate 16 (The Victoria and Albert Museum, London).

I owe a special debt of gratitude to Dr Trân Quang Hai for allowing me to take the photographs which appear as Colour Plates 17 and 19; and to the other musicians from South-East Asia who appear in these pages and have without exception shown a similar patience and helpfulness; to Dr Margaret Waters for permitting me to photograph her bronze drum (Colour Plate 2); to Sir Ralph Verney for permission to photograph the gamelan instruments at Claydon House (Colour Plate 7 and Plate 12); and to Alix Stone for her drawing of a *kacapi* (Plate 19). My thanks are also due to Dr D. A. Swallow of the Indian Department of the Victoria and Albert Museum and to the staff of the India Office in London for their invaluable suggestions concerning pictures.

Contents

I

The Cultural Background

It took the Second World War to bring the term 'South-East Asia' into everyday use. The harsh facts of military invasion had revealed the interdependence of the area embracing what are now the countries of Burma, Thailand, Kampuchea (Cambodia), Laos, Vietnam, Malaysia, Singapore, Brunei, Indonesia, and the Philippines, and had impressed upon the outside world the strategic importance of the region. The lesson, having been painfully learned, was not forgotten.

Tactical considerations alone would therefore be sufficient explanation for the interlocking interests in defence, communications, political alliances, and military alignments which give contemporary South-East Asia a measure of cohesion. But natural conditions, too, endow it with a certain homogeneity: climate, rich agricultural resources, and relatively easy communications (particularly by sea).

No less patent, however, are deep-rooted divisions. Government ranges from chaotic oppression by invading neighbours through varying degrees of despotism by native military cliques and political oligarchies, and subtle shades both of monarchy and of republicanism, to semblances of genuine democracy. Foreign policies are frequently in conflict, determined as they usually are by affiliations with the warring political ideologies of the great power-blocs and, perhaps more cogently, by the economic and military support which ensues. Nor are states conterminous with societies: ethnic, linguistic, and religious groupings flow across national boundaries and become potentially explosive sources of conflict within them. Some areas are almost deserted while others are ruinously over-populated, with appalling congestion a common problem in the cities.

Peasant agricultural communities whose way of life has scarcely changed in centuries coexist with primitive tribes on the one hand and with advanced urban settlements on the other. Gross disparities of personal wealth, educational opportunity, and medical care are so ubiquitous as to be unremarkable.

Earlier travellers from the West, indeed, saw South-East Asia as scarcely more than a vast and ramified backyard to the mainland, a series of appendages to India and, to a lesser extent, to China. Expressions such as 'Further India', 'Greater India', 'East Indies', and 'Indo-China' are indicative. It cannot, of course, be denied that ancient ties with the two immense and older civilizations were fundamental to the shaping and evolution of the region. Indeed, the northern part of what is now Vietnam was, for more than a thousand years until AD 939, under the direct domination of China, and neighbouring territories at various times acknowledged a more or less dependent status. Indian influence, though never the result of military or political domination, was none the less more extensive, pervasive, and persistent.

It was not, however, overwhelming; nor does the beginning of its significant impact, early in the Christian era, represent the introduction of civilization to barbarians. Mass migrations into the region from the south-west corner of China had taken place much earlier, probably around 2500–1500 BC. The details are shadowy, but it is clear that these prehistoric peoples moved gradually southwards following the river valleys, thence along the coasts of the peninsula and to the neighbouring islands. They drove the native inhabitants, mostly pygmy Negritos, into the hills and jungles, and settled as fishermen and rice-farmers. Long before India became a major influence, they had formed well-established communities which in time evolved distinctive civilizations from their shared cultural background. This background included features which were to endure as intrinsic characteristics of the way of life throughout most of

South-East Asia, and of which notable traces still remain. Especially significant is the common inheritance of animistic beliefs, with all their magical and mystical associations, to which later reference will be made.

What might be described as unqualified animism is now to be found only amongst some of the primitive tribes which still subsist in remote districts. Nevertheless, ancient beliefs were not destroyed by the great religious movements—Hindu, Buddhist, Muslim, and Christian—which were to spread throughout the region, but rather were adapted and absorbed. They were at the root of many dramatic and dance forms, ceremonies of ploughing and harvesting, rites of passage, court rituals, and other social conventions which have all, in varying degrees, survived to the present day. They are the source of the respect for local spirits (such as the *phi* in Thailand and the *nat* in Burma) still widely shown even by adherents to later religious orthodoxies. They continue to be revealed in the awe so often inspired by physical objects regarded as having acquired preternatural powers: a category in which, as will be seen in the next chapter, musical instruments are prominent.

The early settlers became the direct ancestors of many of the predominant ethnic groups in South-East Asia, particularly those of Kampuchea, Peninsular Malaysia, and most of Indonesia west of Bali. What is now called Burma and Thailand was to be overrun, many centuries later, by invaders from the north, and it is from these that most of the present inhabitants of that area are descended. Nevertheless, the newcomers to the region were prompt to adopt the culture they found there: a culture which had long been shaped in the matrix of Indian influence.

This influence originated with the establishment of important maritime trading relations sometime around the first century AD, although this does not exclude the probability of earlier contacts both by sea and, in the northern parts, by overland routes. But although merchants no doubt opened the door, it seems certain that it was not they but Brahman priests who were the harbingers of Indian culture, most probably at the direct invitation of local rulers who were seeking a more than *de facto* authority. The Brahmans could provide them with consecration as god-kings validated by the authentic rites of Indian tradition, and they could initiate them into the style of court life appropriate to their new status.

The earliest Buddhist teachers, who began to arrive at much the same time, also focused their attention—at least in the first instance—upon the courts. In their Indian homeland Buddhism and Hinduism were bitterly opposed, but overseas they seem more often than not to have coexisted without difficulty, and even to have been regarded as two aspects of the same thing. Brahman advisers were esteemed officials even in Buddhist courts. Certainly, by the end of the first millennium, evidence abounds of a high degree of syncretism. Carved images of Hindu gods and of the Buddha gaze out from the temple walls of Angkor. A shared belief in reincarnation provided unlimited scope for the central figures—legendary and historical—of both religions to be identified with each other and, what was perhaps more important, with the living monarch. Nor was the religion of the courts out of harmony with the cults of animism and ancestor-worship which remained the everyday beliefs of most of the population. This was entirely characteristic. South-East Asians have always been not only highly selective in their response to the cultures with which they have come into contact, as ready to ignore features they do not want as to seize upon those they do, but also relentless in adapting and building upon what they take.

What, then, were the lasting effects of the gradual permeation of Indian influence throughout almost the whole of the region except the Chinese-dominated north of Vietnam and the Philippines? Even from a purely musical aspect, the political issues already touched upon are far from irrelevant: for, everywhere, the claims of rulers already legitimized by validating doctrines of kingship learnt from India were both buttressed and asserted by ceremonies and rituals of court life. In these music formed an integral part, often in association with other performing arts such as dancing and theatre.

Evidence from iconographical, archaeological, and literary sources shows that instruments of various kinds were introduced from India and were in common use during the early centuries. Some have survived, but many are no longer played. Presumably, Indian music itself was also brought to South-East Asia; but if so, it had little lasting effect: a likely indication that indigenous traditions were already strongly rooted. The Indian style of dancing was certainly imported, as can be seen in countless temple reliefs, and was to form the basis of many distinctive regional styles, but everywhere it was to be transformed almost, though not totally, beyond recognition.

This was not so, however, with the vast corpus of legend which came from India. In particular, the great epic poems, the *Ramayana* and the *Mahabharata*, were to become part of the warp and woof of life: incidents from them are to be seen depicted everywhere, from ancient temples to modern hotels, and they provided the subject-matter for all manner of dramatic forms. It is true that, again, they were transformed and that sometimes they owe their popularity to local accretions rather than to the original narratives themselves, yet fundamentally they became deeply incorporated into social and religious beliefs–even, it should be added, into religious faiths which were yet to arrive.

Of all artistic genres, none owes more to the *Ramayana* and the *Mahabharata* than the shadow-puppet theatre, famous particularly in Java, Bali, Malaysia, and Thailand, but also known elsewhere. Its origins are obscure–it has been suggested that it may have been amongst early cultural imports from India, or that its roots lie further back in primitive animistic rituals of ancestor-worship brought from China or Central Asia. What seems reasonably clear, however, is that it was the characteristically Javanese style, the *wayang kulit*, which spread to other parts of South-East Asia. This is a token of a more general and important fact: that it was the South-East Asians themselves who were largely responsible for the widespread diffusion of cultural elements, sometimes Indian, sometimes indigenous, but most commonly a fusion of the two.

To see evidence for this, it is not necessary to penetrate very deeply into the political history of the region, which in any case is often uncertain in detail. But amongst the unending struggles for predominance and the innumerable shifts of power, some great empires stand out. The extension of their rule, together with its concomitants in trading relations and marriages between royal families, was a prime contributor to cultural diffusion and integration.

As early as the third century AD, a kingdom called Funan began to emerge in present-day Kampuchea. It sent diplomatic missions both to India and to China, and its tentacles stretched down to the Malay peninsula. By the fifth century, the Malays of the south-eastern coast of Sumatra were establishing themselves as shippers and laying the foundations of the control of the strategically important trade routes connecting China with India, Sri Lanka, and Indonesia, which was to lead to the emergence in the seventh century of the powerful maritime empire of Srivijaya. Srivijaya remained a major force until its influence passed to Melaka in the fourteenth century. During most of its existence, it had as a contemporary the greatest of all the historic empires of South-East Asia. This was the splendid empire of the Khmers, a later successor to Funan, consolidated by Jayavarman II. Jayavarman had spent some time at the court of the Sailendra dynasty in Java, conceivably as a hostage. When he came to power in 802, he asserted his independence precisely by adopting the Brahminic cult and practices of kingship which he had learned. It is believed that he also introduced Javanese dance and drama, including possibly the *wayang kulit*. Within a century, his successors had begun work on a new capital at Angkor, whose ruins still reveal it as one of the world's most sublime architectural masterpieces. From Angkor, the power of the Khmer kings reached over much of modern Thailand, Laos, and Vietnam.

When the Khmer empire began its long decline (leading eventually to the abandonment of Angkor in the mid-fifteenth century), the precipitating cause was a series of attacks by the Thais. As a major ethnic group, the Thais, whose origins were in southern China, were relative newcomers in the region. The history of their gradual move southwards and of the ultimate emergence of the modern Thai state does not need to be detailed here, nor that of the even more chequered but very roughly parallel movement of the Tibeto-Burman-speaking people who were the ancestors of the majority group in modern Burma, nor indeed the complex interactions between them and the other ethnic groups, including the Khmers. What should be noted, however, is the remarkable extent to which the conquerors admired and adopted the culture of those they overcame. Following their assaults on Angkor in the fourteenth century, the Thais carried off with them the royal dancers, musicians, actors, and poets. This persistent theme of cultural dissemination was to be continued when the Thais' own capital, Ayutthaya, was destroyed in 1767 and their artists were similarly carried off by Burmese conquerors.

Ancient traditions were overlaid rather than destroyed by later religious movements—movements which were to give rise to some of the images of the region which most readily come to mind: saffron-robed monks silently making their early morning alms-rounds in Thailand and other Buddhist countries, voices of muezzins blaring out from amplifiers high in the minarets of mosques in Malaysia and Indonesia, penitential scourgings and crucifixions in the Philippines. It may appear surprising to mention Buddhism in this context since its early introduction into South-East Asia has already been noted, but a distinction has to be made between the religion of the rulers and their circles on the one hand and that of the mass of the people on the other. The austere tradition of Theravada Buddhism, which was brought from Sri Lanka to Burma and took root there in the twelfth century, was in effect a new religious current—not so much because of its reformist doctrines as because of its zeal as a popular missionary movement addressed to all classes of society. From Burma it quickly spread throughout Thailand, Kampuchea (Cambodia), and Laos and became entrenched.

The later penetration of Islam throughout Malaysia and Indonesia (except Bali) did not begin in earnest until the fifteenth century, although the way had been prepared much earlier by seafaring merchants. It was a gradual and, on the whole, peaceful process which has been described as 'Islamization' rather than conversion. The Sufi tradition was the more readily acceptable because its mystical practices had a temperamental appeal and because it was tolerant, able to reconcile the strict tenets of orthodoxy with local beliefs and customs. Nevertheless, in the wake of strengthening connections in religion and trade came many innovations, not least in the sphere of music. Particularly along some of the coastal areas of Sumatra and other islands, music of Persian and Arabic origin left a lasting impression, and a number of Middle Eastern instruments became established.

The Christian gospel came too late to displace Islam, just as Islam had failed to make any impression where Theravada Buddhism was already established. Only in the Philippines did Christianity become a majority religion, but there the counter-Reformation missionaries who followed in the footsteps of the Spanish conquerors in the sixteenth century found what might almost be described as virgin territory. Although it had for many centuries been host to immigrants from Indonesia, and had had trading connections with China, it had remained in a very real sense on the periphery, producing no kingdoms or empires comparable to Srivijaya or the others with which it had come into contact, relatively little exposed to the Indian influence which had been so potent elsewhere. By the sixteenth century, it is true, Islam had established a toe-hold in the south, but in other parts it had little impact.

Except in the Philippines, early European colonization had but a superficial effect upon the cultural life of South-East Asia, although it is worth noting that some instruments, e.g. the violin and guitar, were quickly naturalized by being accepted into various popular ensembles. Western furnishings and styles of dress became fashionable in the courts and amongst the well-to-do; yet, below the surface, native ways of life often flourished the more for having become symbols of local loyalty. In the nineteenth century courts of Central Java, for example, political impotence went hand in hand with an unprecedented flowering of traditional arts and insistence upon proper ceremony.

The post-colonial exposure to a broader Western influence through films, records, television, radio, mass travel, and all the insidious enticements of coveted technologies is quite a different matter, however. Western popular arts and forms of entertainment are enthusiastically welcomed, and none more than music: even in remote regions, it is almost impossible to be entirely beyond the range of aural equivalents of Coca-Cola. The effects, nevertheless, have been variable. In some places, indigenous musical traditions continue the struggle to survive only through the self-conscious efforts of enthusiasts and occasionally the direct support of government departments, universities, or other official bodies; elsewhere, it is still genuinely rooted in the lives and affections of the mass of the people, even though the very same people may also relish the latest Western imports.

Another type of cultural invasion accelerated rapidly from around the beginning of the nineteenth century with the large-scale immigration of Indian and Chinese workers. The Chinese were the more numerous, but settled communities of both races became established. Some cultural fusion has inevitably occurred, but the immigrant communities have largely preserved and fostered their own, independent traditions. The Chinese opera troupes, which are still to be seen, are a case in point. Such traditions, however, no less than those which are indigenous, are increasingly threatened by the popularity, especially among younger people, of Western music.

2

The Musical Setting

IN a region where historical records of any kind are often thin, easily shading into myth and legend, it is not surprising that little is known of detailed musical history. Yet the intriguing glimpses offered by archaeology, temple reliefs, and painted murals are sufficient to show the importance of music as an everyday activity from very early times. Moreover, they often reveal a close resemblance between instruments still in regular use and those of great antiquity. The sounds that are heard today are themselves historical evidence: the continuing importance of gongs throughout almost the entire area, producing what has been termed the 'gong-culture' of South-East Asia, is a record of ancient migrations and communications; while the presence of instruments from India, China, and the Middle East betrays later movements and contacts.

But what did the music of past ages sound like? What were the musicians perpetuated in stone on the terraces of Angkor or Borobudur, for example, actually playing? Here, one can only speculate. Although the timbre of some ancient instruments can be judged from modern counterparts, there is no certain way of knowing even how they were tuned, let alone the details of the music's construction. Notation, where it exists at all, is rarely much more than a century old, and even then it is but a very partial guide—an *aide-mémoire* to music already known rather than the detailed prescription given by Western scores. Nor are there any theoretical treatises comparable to those in the history of Indian music. Only with the invention of the wax cylinder in the late nineteenth century did the music cease to vanish into thin air.

The widespread distribution of certain instruments may

point to a common stock, but they can scarcely be said to speak a common musical language. Distinctive national and ethnic traditions have evolved, along with endless regional variants and local dialects. Shared technical features do, however, exist, as well as shared perceptions of the nature and function of music: 'South-East Asian music' may be a loose concept, but it implies more than the music found in a particular geographical area.

Not all of its characteristics have an immediate appeal to foreigners, or are readily understood. No platitude is more misleading than that which describes music as an international language. Certainly, early Western travellers were more often than not largely baffled by the music they heard, and their reactions were frequently dismissive. They were not professional musicians, of course; but there is no reason to suppose that, even if they had been, they would have given much better accounts. Here it is illuminating to refer to Dr William Crotch. Crotch, who was born in 1775, was a child prodigy who became Professor of Music at Oxford at the age of twenty-one. A gifted composer, he was also an influential teacher and a musician with a rare breadth of outlook. Through Sir Thomas Stamford Raffles, he was able to make some direct contact with the music of Java. Raffles had imported a large collection of Javanese instruments: those which now form the so-called 'Raffles gamelan' in the British Museum, and the collection at Claydon House in Buckinghamshire (though neither constitutes a complete gamelan—other instruments were lost in a shipwreck). He also brought with him a Javanese aristocrat, Raden Rana Dipura, when he returned to England in 1816. Like many of his class, Raden Rana Dipura seems to have been an amateur musician. There can be little doubt that Crotch was the 'eminent composer' before whom, according to Raffles (1817: 470), he performed 'several of his national melodies' upon the *gambang kayu* (see pp. 39–42). A junior colleague of Raffles, John Crawfurd, recorded that Crotch had examined the collection of instruments as a whole, and moreover had been supplied with 'a variety of airs taken down [in Western notation] by my friend Mr Scott of Java' (Crawfurd, 1820: 333).

Having heard the instruments, Crotch must have been aware that their tunings correspond with no Western tunings and cannot be accurately represented in Western notation. Yet he was content to report that they 'are all in the same kind of scale as that produced by the black keys of the piano-forte' (ibid.: 333). Perhaps he should not be too severely criticized for this: an adequate analytical system had not yet been devised, and he was confronted with the additional problem of explaining technicalities to laymen. But the fact that he could go on to add Western harmonies to some of Scott's versions of Javanese airs can only lead one to marvel at the extent to which the conditioning of his own musical culture had led him to misapprehend one which was strange to him.

Scale systems are in fact amongst the most important features which give the musical traditions of South-East Asia a measure of homogeneity. Generally speaking, seven-note or five-note scales (or both) are the norm, but their constituent intervals are not the exact tones and semitones of Western scales. Both larger and smaller intervals may be used. The two main exceptions to this broad pattern are the Philippines, where Western tunings have largely, though not entirely, displaced scales similar to those found elsewhere in the region, and Vietnam. The Chinese roots of Vietnamese culture have given its music many features which are atypical in South-East Asia as a whole, including a scale of seven notes made up of tones and semitones virtually as in Western music, though evolved independently.

With these two exceptions, it can be said that there is a general resistance to standardization and that, within quite broad limits, tuning is largely a matter of taste. True, there is a tendency towards equidistance–the seven-note scales found in Thailand, Burma, Laos, Kampuchea, and some districts in the Philippines tend to divide the octave into roughly equal intervals, and so does the five-note *slendro* scale of Indonesia–but the individual intervals are not precisely fixed. Neither are they in the seven-note *pelog* scale of Indonesia, which consists of a mixture of large and small intervals whose size can be as much as a minor third in Western terms, or less than a semitone. It is the mixture of large and small intervals which is the essential characteristic of *pelog*, not the seven notes: sometimes fewer are used. In Bali, for example, there are tuning systems which can be regarded as five-note *pelog* (though the terms *slendro* and *pelog* are not ordinarily used there). Even octaves are not always exact, and nor is there any notion of a fixed pitch standard such as the conventional A = 440 of Western music.

None of this implies, however, that South-East Asian musicians are indifferent to niceties of pitch and intonation: far from it. In Java and Bali, the individual tuning of a particular set of gamelan instruments is greatly relished, and it is accepted that a piece which sounds well on one set may not be equally successful on another. Moreover, vocalists and players of instruments (such as strings) which can produce infinite gradations of pitch often make subtle use of minute inflections of notes of the basic scale, either as decorations of them or as alternatives.

Even where seven-note scales are available, most South-East Asian music–including that of Vietnam–is pentatonic, i.e. it uses only five of the notes in the scale. Two notes are therefore ignored altogether, or at least given a markedly subsidiary status. The choice of the particular five notes on which a composition is based, and the relative importance attached to them, are important features in determining its musical flavour: a situation which has some affinities with the modal system of

Gregorian chant and much folk-music in the West. Western folk-music, indeed, is itself frequently pentatonic, as is a great deal of traditional music throughout the world. Thus, although Dr Crotch's specific reference to the black notes of a piano may have been a misleading over-simplification, he was broadly on the right lines when he continued, '... in which scale so many of the Scots and Irish, all the Chinese, and some of the East Indian and North American airs of the greatest antiquity were composed'.

The solecism entailed in his harmonizations of Javanese melodies arises not merely from the fact that the notes of the original scales do not lend themselves to the formation of Western-style chords, but more importantly because all indigenous South-East Asian music is completely non-harmonic in the Western sense. This does not imply that the simultaneous occurrence of two or more different notes is unknown or even unusual. What is lacking, however, is the dimension of harmonic *progression* in Western music: the feeling that one chord leads logically to the next, creating increases of tension or relaxation which, deployed on a large scale, are essential building-blocks in the architecture of the music as a whole.

Much of the music of the region is actually monophonic, i.e. it consists merely of a single line of melody (though not necessarily played by a single instrument), possibly with the addition of a drum accompaniment. But from this simple principle have evolved musical textures (technically known as heterophony) which, at their most sophisticated, notably in the large gamelan orchestras of Central Java, can be extremely rich and ornate.

The foundation of these textures is the spaced-out notes of an outline melody—called *balungan* in Java, *pokok* in Bali—combined with higher-pitched elaborations of the same melody. Elaborations are carried out in various ways: for example, by reiterations of the foundation notes, by ornamenting them with standardized variation patterns, by improvisation in the gaps between them, and by anticipating the next foundation note. The various layers of melody coincide on common notes at important structural points (equivalent to the ends of paragraphs or sentences) in the music. These points are reinforced by cyclic patterns of strokes on various gongs, a system which the West has chosen to call 'colotomy'.

The basis of the rhythmic organization is a simple and regular duple or quadruple metre, which is virtually the rule throughout South-East Asia. Consequently, although drumming patterns, for example, can be intricate, there is nothing in the music comparable to the rhythmic subtleties of Indian music with its complex metres.

Music may not be an international language, but man's instinct for musical expression can truly be said to be universal. Universal, too, are the outlets which this expression finds: in work-songs, laments, serenades, and lullabies; in rituals and ceremonies, both domestic and official; as a spur to battle; as an accompaniment to dancing and an ingredient of dramatic presentations; not least, as a means of simple pleasure and entertainment. All that is unique to South-East Asia is the particular form and character of these outlets.

While they are far too numerous and diverse for a detailed listing here, what may usefully be said is that they are largely conditioned by three features which, to a considerable extent, are consistent throughout the region: the peasant way of life of the majority of its inhabitants, the traditional role of princely courts in promoting the highest artistic standards, and the residual beliefs which form a profoundly important substratum to the established religious orthodoxies, whether Hindu, Buddhist, Muhammadan, or Christian.

It has to be remembered that the music which figures most prominently in the tourist circuits, or, for that matter, which most engages the attention of Western musicians, is not necessarily the most representative. The typical music-maker in South-East Asia is not an urban professional but a rural amateur: a member of a village or peasant community in which traditional music is part of everyday life, which has made its own instruments out of inexpensive materials, whose performing techniques are generally simple but here and there dazzling in both skill and invention.

In the courts, as has already been suggested in Chapter 1, the arts were cultivated from the earliest times not merely as an adornment of kingship but as a validation of it—a tradition which still lingers where the courts themselves have survived. It is possible that in some circumstances royal music even became entirely divorced from that of the masses (the sunset years of the golden period at Angkor may have been an instance); but if this was so it has certainly not been the rule. Javanese courts are not alone in having always been ready to draw on popular material and refine it. More importantly, they have then set standards of performance which, as in so many other areas of behaviour, ordinary people adopted as models to be emulated, in so far as this was possible and appropriate.

The custom of associating certain compositions with particular events, such as the arrival of guests, is commonplace; but it attained a special significance in court life, where some pieces were exclusively reserved to the ruler or his heir apparent. This was a practice which could be much more than a polite convention or mark of respect. There are instances of compositions which are regarded as strictly taboo, such as the music accompanying the *Beḍaya Ketawang* dance at the *kraton* (court) in the Central Javanese city of Surakarta, infringements being an offence against supernatural powers and thus fraught with real danger. Though the *Beḍaya Ketawang* may be an extreme case, it is not an isolated one; and in a looser and more general way, the connection of music with the supernatural is widespread and touches all levels of society. Everywhere it is apparent in ceremonies appropriate to birth, marriage, and death; in rituals for the cure of sickness or for the warding off of ills of all kinds; and in observances marking the agricultural seasons. It is all too easy for outsiders to overlook the serious basis of what may appear to be a mere form of entertainment. Thus hobby-horse dancing, for example, which in the West may be no more than a children's game or a quaint survival of a medieval pastime, is a trance-dance in Java. In Bali and elsewhere, dance may be a preparation for spirit possession.

Perhaps better than any other genre, shadow-puppet plays (whose origins were touched upon on pp. 5–6) demonstrate the integration of art, entertainment, and ancient mystical beliefs only partially tinctured by formal religious creeds, to all of which must be added the inculcation of ethical values and social conventions. *Wayang kulit* performances can always be apprehended at different levels of meaning, and if they are increasingly viewed primarily as sources of entertainment, more profound spiritual and symbolic implications are never wholly absent. The role of its central figure, the *dalang*, is paramount. Not only is he the puppeteer, he also narrates (extempore) the traditional stories, speaks or sings in different voices the words of all the characters, and controls the music provided by the gamelan orchestra and singers ranged behind him (see Colour Plate 1). Traditionally, he prepares for a performance by saying prayers–invocations to Allah and to local spirits, with Brahmin and Buddhist references as well. That he originally had a priestly function as a caller-up of spirits can scarcely be doubted.

The shadow-puppet play is not unique, however. Other types of puppet-theatre and other dramatic forms (notably various traditions of dance-drama) to which music is integral are widespread throughout South-East Asia. It would probably not be too sweeping to say that, in the generality of them, there is a dimension of ancient religious and mystical beliefs expressed in terms of myth, whose continuing acceptance is still often demonstrated by ritual preparations. Old traditions have proved amazingly tenacious in spite of the vast popularity of various new kinds of theatre with more obviously contemporary themes and characters and more naturalistic methods of performance.

The connection of music with the supernatural is frequently apparent in the reverence shown to musical instruments themselves. Thus, the forging of gongs is not merely a manufacturing process but one requiring spiritual preparation and due observance of proper rituals. Particularly if they are of great antiquity or have a special use on solemn occasions such as funeral ceremonies, instruments are widely regarded as having living personalities, as being the habitat of spirit powers. Again, they are surrounded by taboos which, if disregarded, can lead to all kinds of disaster, as many popular stories relate. The custom of honouring or propitiating esteemed instruments with flowers, candles, incense, and other offerings is no less a tradition in Buddhist, Hindu, or Muslim areas than amongst remote tribespeople of less orthodox beliefs.

In Java, sets of gamelan instruments are customarily given poetic proper names, often preceded by the honorific term *Kyahi*. The more august examples, such as those in the courts of Yogyakarta and Surakarta, are venerated as sacred heirlooms (*pusaka*). A similar reverence is paid to the instruments forming the *nobat* ensembles regarded as insignia of royalty in some of the Malaysian courts (see p. 77).

Exposed to Western materialism and rationality, traditional beliefs are sometimes declining in more sophisticated circles. Yet, even here, old ways can be strongly tenacious, if only as a matter of outward observance. For a Javanese musician to step over a gamelan instrument, for example, would still be almost inconceivable. And even though the honouring of such conventions may increasingly denote little more than a regard for custom and a reluctance to offend the susceptibilities of an older generation, at the very least it seems also to express something which will find a sympathetic response from Western musicians, too: an indefinable respect for the means by which music is created.

3

Metal Instruments

WHEN Dr Crotch inspected the Raffles gamelan instruments, he remarked that the tone of 'a pair of gongs, ... suspended from the centre of a most superb wooden stand richly carved, painted, and gilt, ... exceeded in depth and quality any thing I had ever heard' (Crawfurd, 1820: 336). Javanese gongs have remained the special envy of Western composers, though their majestic sounds are but part of the broad spectrum of sonorities produced by the numerous metal percussion instruments of South-East Asia.

These instruments, apart from being the most distinctive and original characteristic of the region's music as a whole, are also one of its most ancient features. Centuries before Indian civilization began to make its indelible mark there, metal-working was already known. No later than 300 BC (some authorities put it much earlier), bronze drums were already amongst the most prominent artefacts of what is known as the Dong-son culture, after a village in the north of Vietnam where its most important traces were discovered. The drums were constructed in various sizes, but were always entirely metal: even the striking surface was made of metal, not skin. They were elaborately decorated, both with abstract geometrical designs and with representations of human and animal life, usually with a star at the centre of the head. Often they are known as 'frog drums' because of the figures of frogs placed as decorations at four equidistant points around the rim. Frogs imply an association with rain-making ceremonies, but an even older use of the drums may have been as signalling instruments.

The early bronze drums were widely distributed throughout South-East Asia, and indeed even further afield. What is most remarkable, however, is that instruments of essentially the same construction, with only minor variations of design, have continued to be made until our own times. Found in Burma (Colour Plate 2), Thailand, Kampuchea, and Laos, they are principally associated with the Karen (a tribal group living in the mountainous region between Burma and northern Thailand), amongst whom they have immense prestige since they are believed to be invested with magic powers. These powers are of profound importance in the cycle of agricultural activities, as well as in funeral rites and ceremonies for the summoning of ancestor spirits. Elsewhere, bronze drums are no longer used: with very few exceptions, the present-day drums are made of wood (see Chapter 4).

The majority of metal instruments in current use fall into one of three categories: (1) gongs (of various kinds), (2) cymbals, and (3) metal-bar instruments. Bronze is still by far the most common metal, with a basic mixture of ten parts copper to three of tin (the precise formula being a jealously guarded secret of the gong-smiths). As an economy measure, iron is sometimes substituted, and for special purposes, brass and other alloys are also used. The bronze drums discussed above have always been cast, but gongs and related instruments are forged: molten metal is shaped by a long process of alternate hammering and re-heating (Colour Plate 3). The 'keys' of instruments such as the *saron* (see pp. 33–4) are roughly formed in moulds, and then cold-hammered. Fine-tuning is achieved by filing. Periodic adjustments are normally needed for several years after an instrument has been taken into use, but once it has settled down, little further attention is necessary.

The Gong Family

'Gong' is one of the few words of Javanese/Malay origin to have been absorbed into the English language. Yet although the instrument is so strongly identified with South-East Asia, it probably did not originate there but was introduced from or via China. Nevertheless, the evidence suggests that in Java, where they have been most fully developed, gongs have been used since at least the ninth century. They exist in a wide variety of shapes and sizes. Most produce a note of definite pitch, unlike the Western orchestral tam-tam or the gongs used in Chinese opera. An almost universal feature is a central boss, where the instrument is struck with a padded beater. Flat gongs, however, are also found, e.g. in some districts of the Philippines.

The largest gongs are suspended vertically (see Plate 1 for an exceptionally large and fine example). In static ensembles, they

1. Temple gong, cast in 1860, at Wat Phrathat Haripunchai in Lamphun, northern Thailand.

are hung from wooden stands, normally placed behind the other instruments; in procession, they are hung from a wooden pole borne between the shoulders of two men. Smaller instruments may be carried in one hand and beaten with the other. Horizontally played gongs are generally somewhat more elaborately shaped than the suspended gongs, often with rims which are proportionately much deeper. Individual instruments of this kind are often described as 'pot gongs' or 'gong-kettles'.

Reference was made on p. 16 to the cyclic patterns of gong strokes used in gamelan music. The gong which marks out the longest musical periods is also the largest in size and hence the deepest in sound: the 'great gong'—the *gong ageng* or *gong geḍe* of Central Java and Bali (Plate 2 and Colour Plate 7). Typically, its diameter is 70–100 cm and its weight about 22–32 kg (though some examples are more than twice as heavy), with a pitch around 35–45 Hz, i.e. in the region of the lowest

2. Rack of gongs in modern Javanese gamelan, including *kempul* and (on the right) a *gong ageng*, with a *kendang* (drum) below.

notes of the double bass. Like the other gongs, it is never violently struck, but its rich, deep resonance is unmistakable even in the largest and most elaborate gamelans.

A similar but slightly smaller gong is the *gong suwuk* or *gong siyem* of Central Java, which has a subsidiary role as a punctuating instrument, or may even replace the *gong ageng* in smaller compositions. Also similar, but even smaller, is the *kempul* (Plate 2), used throughout Java, and its Balinese equivalent, the *kempur*. In the very large gamelan orchestras of Central Java, the number of *kempul* has steadily increased from one or two in the nineteenth century to as many as nine or even more, tuned to the notes of both the *slendro* and the *pelog* scales. (Gamelan orchestras may consist exclusively of sets of instruments tuned to either system, but the largest ensembles, in Central Java, are double gamelans with two independent sets of instruments, one for each, though the two are never played simultaneously.)

Similar suspended gongs are used throughout the region. In Thailand and Laos, for example, the *khǭng mōng* (Plates 3 and

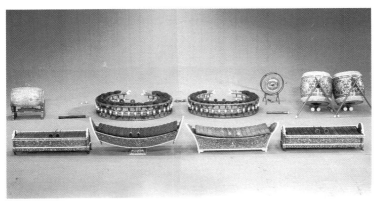

3. Instruments of a Thai *pī phāt* ensemble. From left to right: front row—*ranāt ēk lek, ranāt ēk, ranāt thum, ranāt thum lek*; back row—*taphōn, pī nai* (*ching* behind), *khǭng wong yai, chāp lek, khǭng wong lek, khǭng mōng, pī nḡk*, a pair of *klǭng that*.

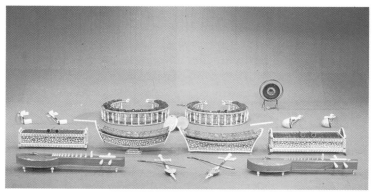

4. Instruments of a Thai *mahōrī* ensemble. From left to right: front row—
two *čhakhē* and two *sǭ sām sāi* (in centre); middle row—*ranāt ēk lek*, *ranāt*
ēk, *ranāt thum*, *ranāt thum lek*, back row—two *sǭ duang*, *khlui*, (*ching*
behind), *khǭng wong yai*, *rammanā*, *thōn*, (*chāp* behind), *khǭng wong lek*,
khlui, (*khǭng mōng* behind), two *sǭ ū*.

4, and Colour Plate 6) resembles the *kempul*, though it is not
tuned to a definite pitch. There are suspended gongs with
much deeper rims, such as the *tawak* found in the *kulintang*
ensembles of the Philippines and parts of the island of Borneo,
and in Sumatra and Peninsular Malaysia.

The *kenong* is another punctuating instrument in Javanese
gamelan, and the largest of the individual pot gongs (see Plate 15
and Colour Plate 23). A gamelan made up of both *slendro* and
pelog instruments might include four or five *kenong* tuned to
notes of the *slendro* scale and five to seven tuned to *pelog* notes.
Each is supported on diagonally crossed cords in a rectangular
frame holding one to three gongs. Similarly supported are two
smaller pot gongs also used as colotomic instruments: the *ketuk*
and *kempyang* (Plate 15), the former being a little smaller and
flatter than the latter. One or possibly two of each are used in
each of the two tuning systems.

Sets of small pot gongs are ubiquitous throughout the

region, almost invariably grouped together in wooden frames of various kinds. What may be an older arrangement is represented in East Javanese temple reliefs of the thirteenth and fourteenth centuries showing an instrument shaped like a dumb-bell, consisting of a wooden bar with a small bossed gong attached to each end, lying across the player's lap. Such an instrument, the *reyong*, has survived until modern times, notably in Bali, played either seated or carried in procession (suspended by a cord passed around the neck), but in either case normally used in pairs, with two performers playing interlocking patterns on the four gongs. This type of *reyong*, however, has been largely superseded by one in which the gongs rest on cords in a rack, laid out horizontally and in line. Originally the horizontal *reyong* also included four gongs and was still played by two men, but under the influence of the new *kebyar* style (see p. 70), the number of gongs was increased during the 1930s to eight or even twelve, requiring three or four players (Colour Plate 21). Twelve-gong *reyong* provide a range of two and a half octaves.

Sets of small gongs of this kind forming a complete or nearly complete scale constitute a category known in the West as 'gong-chimes', though the term is also applied to similar scalic groups of small suspended gongs, such as the *jengglong* used in Sundanese gamelan. Instruments in this category are concerned with melody: normally, with highly elaborate decorations of the basic melody. Thus, even the largest collections of *kenong* are not included because of their different, i.e. colotomic, function.

Balinese gamelan provides another example of gong-chimes: the *trompong*, a two-octave set of horizontal gongs similar in appearance to the *reyong* but played by a single musician, to whom it offers challenging opportunities for virtuoso improvisation (Plate 5). Two versions of the instrument may be used, in which case the principal one is the *trompong pengarap*

5. The *trompong* is a gong-chime with a two-octave range used in Balinese *gamelan gong*. It is played with a high degree of display as a vehicle for solo, melodic improvisation.

(or *trompong gede*), to distinguish it from the subsidiary *trompong barangan*, pitched an octave higher.

As in the modern *reyong*, the *trompong*'s pots are laid out in a single row. This arrangement is widely used, e.g. in the variously sized *kulintang* gong-sets (Plate 6) from which the *kulintang* ensembles already mentioned take their name. The *bonang* belonging to archaic forms of gamelan in Java (the *gamelan munggang*, *koḍok ngorek*, and *carabalen*—see p. 79) provide another example of sets of gong-kettles arranged in the same way. But other distributions, too, are found. The *bonang* in Sundanese-speaking areas of West Java are set out in two rows of gongs at right angles to each other. The modern gamelan of Central Java includes two versions of the *bonang* (the *bonang barung* and, an octave higher, the *bonang panerus*); both consist of double rows of gongs, one laid behind the other in the same frame (Plates 7 and 8).

6. Philippine *kulintang* (gong-chime).

7. Javanese *bonang* player. (The photograph was taken in London in November–hence the gloves!)

8. *Bonang* with one of the pots removed.

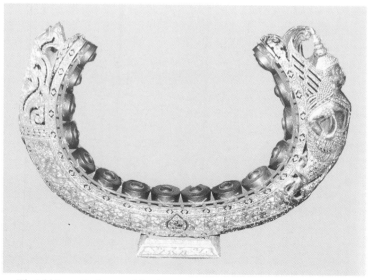

9. Thai *khǭng mǭn* (gong-chime).

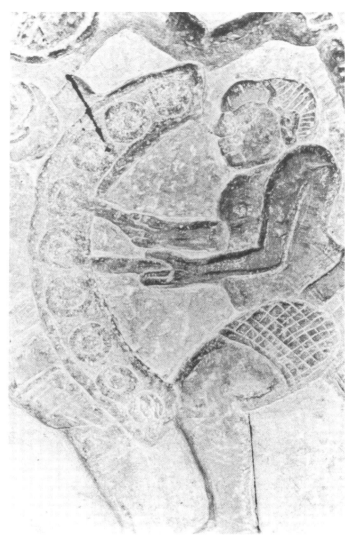

10. Khmer gong-chime: detail of a carving at Angkor Wat (twelfth century).

Thailand, Burma, Kampuchea, and Laos offer two different arrangements: (1) an almost-closed circle of gongs, e.g. the *khǭng wong* in Thailand (Plates 3, 4, and 24 and Colour Plate 6) and the Burmese *kyì-waìng* (Colour Plate 12); (2) an upright horse-shoe shape, as in the Thai *khǭng mǭn* (Plate 9)—not to be confused with the *khǭng mōng* mentioned earlier. These instruments, too, exist in versions tuned an octave apart, e.g. the *khǭng wong yai* and the smaller *khǭng wong lek*. Their family resemblance to arc-shaped racks of gongs carved on Angkor Wat in the first half of the twelfth century is striking (Plate 10).

Cymbals

Similar reliefs on even older shrines in Java, notably the vast Buddhist monument of Borobudur (completed during the first half of the ninth century), provide evidence of the early use of cymbals. Among the many examples illustrated in a number of scenes depicted there, two principal types may be distinguished, often described as rim-shaped and cup-shaped respectively. It has been variously claimed that cymbals originated in China, India, or Turkey; certainly they are of very great antiquity, as Middle Eastern representations of them dating from before the first millennium testify.

Western orchestral cymbals are examples of the rim-shaped category, although South-East Asian versions are always smaller, with a narrower rim, and the rounded boss at the centre proportionately larger. An example is the Thai *chāp*, a pair of cymbals used mainly in large ensembles (Plates 3 and 4). *Chāp* are made in two sizes: the *chāp lek*, typically with a diameter of 12–14 cm and—approximately twice as big—the less common *chāp yai*.

Similar pairs of cymbals are common in many other parts of South-East Asia, generally played with one held face upwards and the other clashed face downwards on to it. In Bali, where they are called *ceng-ceng* (a term also applied there to cymbals

32

in general), they are frequently used in sets: possibly as many as six or even more pairs of instruments in different sizes (typically 15–25 cm in diameter) which play interlocking rhythmic patterns. When seated, a performer may play two pairs: two instruments placed on the ground being struck from above by two held in the hands. This last method of playing is also used for the much smaller *rincik*, in which the upward-facing cymbals, either a pair or two overlapping groups of three, are mounted on a wooden base.

Cup-shaped cymbals are generally small and rimless. A very common example in Thailand and the neighbouring countries is the *ching*: a pair of tiny cymbals (about 6 cm in diameter) made of thick metal and joined by a cord knotted inside a hole at each of their apexes (Plate 4). One of the pair is cupped in the left hand and struck by the other.

Metal-key Instruments

The 'keys' of the South-East Asian metal-key instruments are in fact a series of oblong plates or slabs of metal supported in a wooden frame. They are arranged scale-wise and are struck with various kinds of beater. Two types may be distinguished: (1) thick metal slabs, usually slightly arched along their length, the largest sometimes bossed in the centre, and (2) thin metal plates, bevelled at the edges. Both are employed in Javanese and Balinese gamelan, the former typified by the *saron* and the latter by the *gender*.

Normally *saron* (Colour Plates 7, 22 and 23) have five to seven heavy metal slabs as their keys, covering a range of approximately an octave, but more extensive instruments are also found, particularly in West Java. (A multi-octave form in Central Java, the *gambang gangsa*, is now virtually obsolete.) The keys are laid horizontally on a wooden trough; each is supported by a thin cushioning of soft material, and held in place by holes at its two ends which slot on to nails protruding perpendicularly from the trough. Underneath the row of keys, a cavity gouged out of the wood acts as a resonator. In performance, the keys are struck singly with a mallet made of wood or buffalo horn held in the player's right hand. As each key is struck, the one before it is simultaneously damped by the fingers of the left hand.

Saron are made in various sizes. In modern Central Javanese gamelan, for example, three forms are generally used; from lowest to highest they are the *saron demung* (or just *demung*), *saron barung*, and *saron panerus* or *peking*. Even moderately sized gamelan ensembles generally include several of each, playing in unison: they are the basic melodic instruments in the musical texture since their function is to play the outline of the underlying melody.

Like those of the *saron*, the *gender*'s keys are arranged horizontally, but the thin metal plates are laced together and suspended in a case over individual resonating tubes made of bamboo or tin. Earlier Javanese *gender* were built taller than their modern counterparts (compare Plates 11 and 12). The range of the latter normally extends over two or more octaves: it is true that single-octave versions of the same instrument are used (see below), but they have a different musical function and are not generally termed *gender*.

Large Central Javanese gamelan include *gender* at two different pitches–the *gender barung* and the subsidiary *gender panerus*, pitched an octave higher. There are three of each, used singly: one in *slendro* and two alternative versions for different modes of the *pelog* tuning. Modern instruments usually have fourteen keys. They are played with a pair of light mallets with padded, disc-shaped heads, one in each hand; and they elaborate the texture with a delicate tracery of intricate variations upon the basic melody. The *slentem* is in effect a large, one-octave *gender* (in some districts it is known as *gender panembung*), but it is played with a single beater and merely doubles the unadorned version of the outline melody an octave below the *saron*

11. Modern Javanese *gender*.

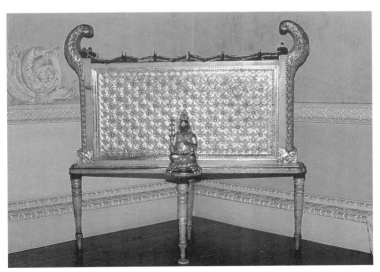

12. Old-fashioned (tall) *gender*. At Claydon House in Buckinghamshire, England.

demung. Bali offers a wide range of *gender* types, mention of which will be made in Chapter 6 in connection with different forms of Balinese gamelan.

Around the mid–nineteenth century, two metal-key instruments were devised in Thailand and introduced into large ensembles there and in Kampuchea: the *ranāt ēk lek* and a lower-pitched version, the *ranāt thum lek* (Plates 3 and 4). Both were adaptations of an older, xylophone-type instrument (i.e. with wooden keys), the *ranāt ēk* (see pp. 39–40), but the inspiration to use metal keys probably came from the Indonesian *gambang gangsa* and *gender*, with both of which they have features in common. Like the *gender*, both are multi-octave instruments which play variation patterns with two disc-headed beaters. The keys, however, are too heavy to be suspended, and thus are supported on the box, which acts as a resonator.

Others

Metal instruments not belonging to the above categories are to be found in South-East Asia, but they are comparatively rare— or rather, they are rarely used as *musical* instruments. Bells of many kinds, for instance, appear in the reliefs at Borobudur and elsewhere, and they are still a regular feature of everyday life: temple bells, both large and small; hawkers' bells; cattle bells; handbells used in religious devotions and shamanistic rituals. Yet, as instruments in organized musical ensembles, they are unusual. An example, however, is the bell-tree (a cluster of tiny bells hanging at different levels from supports attached to a central upright stick), which produces a continuous jingle when shaken. It is occasionally heard in certain types of gamelan in Bali, and in some archaic Javanese gamelans. Another rarity is the *kemanak* in Java (*gumanak* in Bali)—a pair of hollow, banana-shaped instruments which are struck one against the other, or played by two players with mallets.

4
Wooden Percussion Instruments and Drums

BECAUSE wood[1] is an accessible and adaptable material, there can be little doubt that people used it to make musical instruments long before they acquired skills in metal-working. It seems reasonable to assume a great antiquity for an instrument as rudimentary as the *krap* of Thailand and Kampuchea: merely two short pieces of wood which are struck together (Colour Plate 6). Variations on this theme include scraping one stick along the notched edge of another. Stamping-sticks or -tubes are another basic device, consisting simply of wooden staves or hollow bamboo tubes held upright and pounded on the ground, or against another object, such as a stone or a hollowed-out log. Yet another elementary contrivance was noted by Henry Yule in the mid-nineteenth century when he observed 'several clappers of split bamboo which make themselves heard, in excellent time, but always too liberally' among the instruments of 'a full Burmese orchestra' (Yule, 1858: 14; Colour Plates 12 and 13). And, even if it is somewhat different in principle, mention may be made here of the jew's harp, a primitive instrument commonly made of bamboo (though metal versions are also used), and widely popular in courting (Colour Plate 8).

The use of cutting and carving to adjust the pitch produced by a piece of wood when struck can be seen in a simple form in the *tagunggak*, played in Sabah. It is merely a length of bamboo tubing, open at the top but closed by a natural node

[1] Unless specifically distinguished, 'wood' may be taken to include bamboo in what follows, although, strictly, bamboo is 'a gigantic tropical and sub-tropical grass with hollow-jointed woody stem' (*Chambers Twentieth Century Dictionary*).

at the bottom, with one side cut away for about half its length at the upper end. Elaborate musical patterns become possible when each of the members of a group plays a differently pitched instrument. Edward M. Frame records that 'In the Dusan areas of the State... the number of tubes is often limited to six or seven, but in the Murut communities the number often approaches forty... with the tube length varying from seven or eight inches to eight or ten feet' (Frame, 1982: 254-5).

In many parts of Indonesia, as well as in Malaysia and Thailand, bamboo tubes—generally two or three—are loosely contained in a wooden frame so that they can be shaken by hand, producing a type of rattle called an *angklung* (Colour Plate 9). Each *angklung* produces only one basic note, with the other tubes tuned to its octaves. Each performer plays an instrument or two (with one in each hand), but a group of performers with differently pitched instruments can produce music of some complexity, using a technique resembling that of Western handbell ringing. *Angklung* of this kind are especially associated in Java with hobby-horse dancing.

Sets of tuned bamboo tubes or slabs of wood are also grouped together so that they can be played by one person using beaters. One arrangement consists of a suspended group of tubes or slabs arranged horizontally and linked together like a rope ladder. The lower end is attached to the knee or foot of the performer (allowing him to pull it slightly towards him as he sits cross-legged facing it), or to his waist, if standing. In Indonesia, bamboo-tube instruments of this kind are called *calung*, though the name is also applied to variations of the same principle, including an instrument in which the two ends of the ropes are tied to the sides of a bowed frame with the linked tubes suspended horizontally between (the *gambang calung*). Other related instruments have bamboo tubes resting directly on a frame, generally angled slightly towards the performer: examples include the *grantang* in Bali (Plate 13), and one in the

1. The *dalang* at a Javanese *wayang kulit* (shadow-puppet theatre) performance combines the roles of puppeteer, narrator, solo singer, and musical director. Up to about 60 two-dimensional puppets may be used during the course of a single performance, held between the overhead lamp and the screen, on to which they project a shadow. The audience may sit on either side of the screen.

2. Bronze drum, popularly known as a 'frog drum' after the frogs around the rim. The instrument illustrated comes from the Karen people of Burma and is relatively modern (nineteenth century?), but very similar drums have been made since about 400 BC.

3. Gong-making at a factory near Surakarta, Central Java.

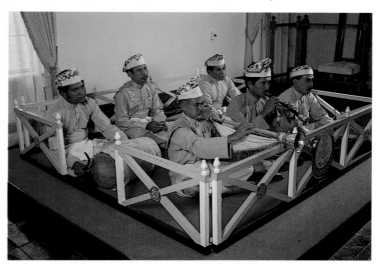

4. The *nobat* ensemble of the royal court of Perak in Peninsular Malaysia. Instruments which can be clearly seen are, in front, the long silver trumpet (*nafiri*) and an oboe (*serunai*), and at the left of the back row, a small drum (*gendang*).

5. A Javanese *wayang golek* performance—broadly similar to the shadow theatre, but using three-dimensional puppets.

6. Malaysian and Thai postage stamps depicting traditional instruments.

7. A group of seven *saron* with two *gong ageng* at Claydon House in Buckinghamshire, England. These are among the instruments which Raffles took to England in 1816.

8. The jew's harp is an instrument popular in many forms throughout South-East Asia. This example is a *kubing* from the southern Philippines.

9. A group of Sundanese *angklung* players: early nineteenth-century coloured drawing from the Mackenzie Collection [f. 89 (100)] in the India Office Library, London.

10. A *silingut* (nose flute) from Sarawak, Malaysia.

11. *Rebana*: frame drums at the drum festival in Kota Bharu, Peninsular Malaysia.

12. A musical scene from an album of six Burmese paintings depicting royal entertainments and ceremonies; probably c.1930s. (By courtesy of the Trustees of the Victoria and Albert Museum, London.)

13. Another scene from the same album.

14. Detail from a carved relief on the temple at Borobudur (ninth century) showing a transverse-flute player.

15. Bamboo trumpets (*kata batang*) and flutes from Sabah, Malaysia.

16. A musician from Northeast Thailand, wearing traditional dress (now quite rare), plays the *khāēn* or bamboo mouth-organ.

17. *Dan tranh*: a Vietnamese zither, played by Dr Trân Quang Hai.

18. Thai ladies playing (from left to right) a *thōn*, *rammanā*, *khlui*, *krajappī*, and *sǭ sām sāi*. Not only the instruments but also the grouping and the postures of the players are identical with those in a stone carving of the Sukhothai period (*c*.1238–1438) illustrated in Morton, 1979: 103.

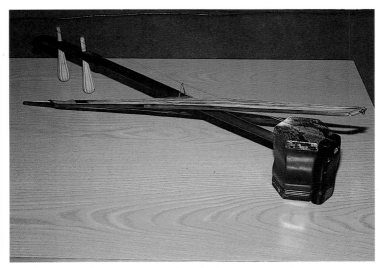

19. *Dan nhi*: a Vietnamese two-string fiddle.

20. Burmese harp (*saùng-gauk*), played by U Myint Maung.

21. Balinese gamelan rehearsal at the senior conservatory for traditional music (ASKI) in Surakarta, Central Java, where all types of gamelan are studied. On the left can be seen the end of a modern *reyong*, in the centre the characteristically Balinese *kendang*, and on the right a group of *gangsa* players.

22. Javanese gamelan players. The four musicians in the front are playing *saron* (tuned to the *pelog* scale); the *slendro* instruments are on their right). Behind them are two *kendang* (drums) and two *celempung* (zithers). At the very top of the picture is a row of *wayang kulit* puppets.

23. Overhead view of a Javanese gamelan at a *wayang golek* performance. The square in the right half of the picture is formed by four *bonang* (two *slendro* and two *pelog*); behind them are the *kenong*. Opposite them, in the left-hand side of the picture, are several *saron* and (in front of the red *kendang*) a *gender*, with a *slentem* by its side; there is another *gender* at the bottom. In the upper part of the picture is a rack of suspended gongs, and in front of them a group of singers.

13. Balinese *grantang* (xylophones).

Banyuwangi district of East Java which is known locally as an *angklung*, though generally referred to elsewhere as a 'Banyu-wangi *angklung*' to distinguish it from the rattle mentioned earlier. In districts where bamboo is used—with remarkable ingenuity—to provide imitations of the prohibitively costly metal instruments of the gamelan, a horizontal row of struck bamboo tubes provides an effective substitute for the *saron*.

Clearly, instruments such as these are akin to the Western orchestral xylophone in their essential principles. The xylo-phone is, in fact, a genus occurring in endless species, not only throughout South-East Asia but in other parts of the world, particularly in Africa. The most sophisticated examples in South-East Asia are the Thai *ranāt ēk* and the Javanese *gambang kayu*. The *ranāt ēk* is a three-octave instrument with keys laced together and hung over a wooden, boat-shaped box which acts as a resonator. Its curved base is supported at the centre on a small pedestal (Plates 3 and 4 and Colour Plate 6). The keys

39

themselves are made either of hardwood or, more traditionally, of bamboo, which is still often preferred for its mellower, if softer, sound. They are graduated in size and chiselled underneath to achieve the basic tunings; fine adjustments are made by applying a mixture of beeswax and lead shavings. Two light sticks are used in performance, with padded knobs at the ends or, when played out of doors, sometimes with hard knobs.

A slightly lower-pitched version of the same instrument, the *ranat thum*, is thought to have been consolidated as recently as the nineteenth century. Apart from a flat base, it is similar in appearance to the *ranāt ēk*, but slightly larger, with longer and wider keys (Plates 3 and 4 and Colour Plate 6). Both instruments are also found in Kampuchea, while the Burmese *pat-talà*, though possessing a rather wider range, is otherwise virtually identical to the *ranāt ēk* (Plate 14).

14. Burmese *pat-talà*: engraving from Yule, 1858: 15.

The Javanese *gambang kayu* differs in that its keys are not suspended but rest directly on the sides of a wooden trough-resonator, supported by small cushions and held in place by nails (Plate 15). Modern examples usually have a four-octave range, though older instruments were rather more limited. The keys are scarcely ever made from bamboo (except sometimes in the villages), various hardwoods being preferred. The instrument is played with a pair of long, thin sticks which have a padded disc at the end. A large gamelan includes three *gambang kayu*, one tuned to *slendro* and two to alternative *pelog* modes.

The two sticks required by multi-octave xylophones such as the *gambang kayu* and the *ranāt ēk* are generally held an octave apart, used with considerable virtuosity to perform elaborate passages in octaves, or elaborations of what are basically octave passages. An unusual extension of the same principle is found

15. Javanese gamelan instruments: in the centre, a *gambang kayu*; behind it, a group of *kenong* to the left and a *kempyang* and *ketuk* to the right.

41

in the Balinese *gamelan gambang* ensembles (see p. 77), in which the xylophone (*gambang*) players are able to produce not two but four octaves simultaneously, by means of a pair of Y-shaped sticks, each with two heads. For reasons of playing technique, the keys are not laid out in an entirely scalic order, and thus appear in what seems to be a haphazard arrangement of lengths and sizes. This relatively complicated type of xylophone is not, as might have been assumed, a recent development: an exactly similar instrument, complete with forked sticks, appears in relief on the Panataran temple in East Java, completed about AD 1375.

Drums

The usual musical meaning of 'drum' is an instrument in which a skin (or, in the West, a synthetic substitute) is tightly stretched across some kind of cavity so as to cover it completely. Opposite the skin, the cavity may be closed (e.g. if it is bowl-shaped), or open, or it may be covered by a second skin.

By this definition, some of the so-called 'drums' of South-East Asia are not drums at all. The bronze drum mentioned on pp. 21–2 is an example, for it is not a 'membranophone', i.e. its striking surface is not made of skin. Similarly excluded are the various types of 'slit-drum', formed by cutting or burning a slit in the side of a hollow piece of wood, as in the Balinese *kulkul*. Slit-drums are in fact more commonly used for signalling than for strictly musical purposes, though even in the former role they include an enormous range, from hollowed-out tree trunks to small, hand-held instruments.

True drums, however, abound: indeed, there can be few musical contexts in which they are not heard. Almost without exception they have a wooden shell, but their numerous and subtle variations of shape often defy exact classification, and commonly used terms such as 'cylindrical', 'conical', or 'barrel-shaped' can rarely be applied without qualification. One drum which really does resemble a barrel, however, is the Thai *klǭng that*, a double-headed drum with identically sized heads (about 46 cm in diameter), whose gently curved sides (about 51 cm long) are widest in the middle. Its hollow body is made from hardwood, with a highly polished or, sometimes, decorated surface. Cow or buffalo hide is used for the skins, cut so as to overlap the ends, each fastened by closely positioned tacks which form a border around the circumference. For performance, one head is placed face downwards, and the body is then tilted towards the player, where it is held in position by an arrangement of crossed poles inserted through a ring set into its back. The player beats upon the upper head with a pair of bamboo sticks. Until the early nineteenth century, only one *klǭng that* was used in *pī phāt* ensembles (see p. 71), but since then two have been usual, tuned to contrasted though not precise pitches (Plates 3 and 24). As with many other pairs of contrasted-pitch instruments elsewhere in the region, the higher-pitched instrument is regarded as 'male' and the lower as 'female'. Tuning is effected by the application of a thick paste made from ashes and cooked rice at the centre of the lower head. A roughly half-sized version of the same drum is also made–the *klǭng chātrī*, used in pairs to accompany the itinerant theatrical form, the *lakhǭn chātrī*.

Similar drums are also found in China. They may even have originated with the early Thai people of its southern borders, and been taken with them on their southern migration. Although in Kampuchea and other mainland countries such drums are widely played, elsewhere in the region they are less common. An example, however, is the *beḍug*, used in Central Java. Usually rather larger than the *klǭng that* and sometimes very much larger, it is suspended horizontally from a wooden frame, and played with a single wooden mallet.

Another barrel-shaped drum in Thailand and neighbouring

countries, the *taphōn*, is differently constructed, and probably
of Indian origin. The edges of the two skins are sewn with
twisted strips of cane which provide the anchorages for leather
thongs running along the length of the drum, pulling the
strings tight. Many thongs are used, covering the shell entirely,
and interwoven by others forming a strip at right angles around
the central bulge. The drum rests horizontally on a stand,
played with the hands on both heads (Plates 3 and 24). It is not
actually quite symmetrical, since one head is slightly larger
than the other (about 25 and 22 cm respectively, with a body
length of about 48 cm). More obviously asymmetrical is the
larger *taphōn mǭn* (corresponding measurements are about
50, 37, and 75 cm). A drum with the same general construction as the *taphōn* except that it is practically cylindrical is the
sǭng nā. All three drums are tuned with a paste mixture, like
the *klǭng that*.

What appear to be drums of the *taphōn* type appear in the
carvings at Angkor Wat. Some three centuries earlier, drums
of many different shapes were portrayed at Borobudur,
amongst them instruments which are still the regular drums
of Indonesia and Malaysia. Most of these have two features in
common. The first is that they are double-headed and normally
played with the hands (though a stick is sometimes held in the
right hand for some of the larger versions); the second is their
method of fastening and tuning the skins, which distinguishes
even the barrel-shaped versions from the Thai *klǭng that* and
taphōn. Such drums are known generally by the generic term
kendang, with or without qualification. Many other spellings
may be found, including *kendang* (*kendhang*) in Java and *gendang* elsewhere, although there are regions where such variants
refer to single-headed drums (e.g. the *gandang* played by some
ethnic groups in Sabah).

Outwardly at least, the Balinese *kendang* represents the species
at its simplest since it is very nearly cylindrical, although taper-

ing slightly at one end, with one head a little smaller than the other (Colour Plate 21). Inside, it is more intricate than its exterior betrays, being carved in an hourglass shape. Like other *kendang*, the Balinese drums are often made from jack-fruit wood, generally with cow or buffalo hide for the skins. Each skin is stretched and held in position by a rattan hoop at the rim, and the two hoops are laced together by strings of rattan or leather. These form a series of N-shaped patterns around the smaller drums; larger drums have Y-shaped patterns formed by pairs of strings being bound together by sliding knots which are used to adjust the tuning. If the player is seated, the drum is positioned in his lap; in procession, it is suspended from his neck. Normally the drums are played in pairs, the larger (*wadon*) being 'female' and the smaller (*lanang*) 'male' again.

Javanese *kendang*, of which there are several versions, can be broadly divided into two main shapes. Both have differently sized heads, tuned to different pitches. Drums in the first category have a modified barrel form: the widest point of the bulge is not at the centre but at a point about a quarter of the way along the side (Colour Plate 22). In the modern gamelan ensembles of Central Java, several different kinds are used, the principal being the *kendang ageng* (or *kendang gending*), played either alone or, by the same person, in partnership with the smaller *kendang kalih* (or *kendang ketipung*). Typical measurements are 80 × 40 × 25 and 44 × 20 × 16 cm respectively. The larger drum rests horizontally on a stand in front of the seated player; if the *kendang kalih* is used, it is placed on his lap. Intermediate sizes include the *kendang wayangan* (reserved for *wayang kulit* performances) or *kendang batangan*, and the rather smaller *kendang ciblon*—a bright-sounding drum associated with a virtuoso style of playing which is especially relished in dramatic contexts.

The other basic shape of Javanese *kendang* is often described as a truncated cone, i.e. resembling an ice-cream cornet with the tip sliced off. In Central Java, such 'conical' drums have been generally superseded by the barrel-shaped drums described above, though they can still be found in archaic forms of gamelan (see p. 79), where they are known as *kendang peneteg*. Conical drums are more common in West Java, although the instruments used in current Sundanese forms of gamelan tend to approximate more closely to the modern barrel shapes of Central Java. They exist in two sizes: *kendang ageung*, the larger, and *kendang leutik* or *kulanter*. The *kendang ageung* rests lengthwise on a stand, but tilted with one end on the floor so that the player can make pitch adjustments with his heel pressed against the drumhead.

Javanese and Balinese *kendang* forms are also used in other countries, their provenance often admitted by their names. Thus, the Malaysian *gendang Jawa* is a drum of the Javanese *kendang ageng* type. The Thai *klǫng khaēk*, though also known as *klǫng chawā* (Javanese drum), is in fact a *kendang* of the type now associated with Bali and, like the latter, exists in 'female' and 'male' versions.

Drums in three other common shapes are generally described as 'long', 'goblet', and 'hourglass' drums. Long drums, mostly found in rural communities, consist of a hollowed-out length of a slender tree trunk, closed at one end, with the skin (often snake skin) at the other end attached by rattan laces. 'Goblet' drums, a type particularly important in Arab countries, are most common, in South-East Asia, in southern Thailand and neighbouring countries. They resemble an inverted vase, with inwardly sloping sides widening slightly at the bottom to form a small base, and bulging out into a bowl at the top (Colour Plates 12 and 18). The skin is stretched over the bulge. Drums meeting this general description exist in many sizes and shapes. An idea of their variety can be gained by comparing typical diameter and height measurements of three Thai drums: *thōn chātrī*, 20 × 36 cm; *klǫng yāo*, 21 × 75 cm *klǫng āe*, 50 × 300 cm. All are made of wood, but another goblet drum, the *thōn mahōrī* (similar in appearance to the *thōn chātrī*) has a body made of ceramic or pottery.

The body of an 'hourglass' drum has a narrow central waist, with a skin covering one or both of its ends. Drums of this kind are less common in South-East Asia than in other parts of the East (e.g. Korea and Japan). Moreover, when a single-headed waisted drum has one end smaller than the other, it can of course be a moot point whether to describe it as hourglass- or goblet-shaped. Thus the *gedumbak* of northern Peninsular Malaysia is often categorized as an hourglass drum although it is equivalent to the Thai *thōn chātrī*.

A different type of construction to that employed in the drums mentioned thus far is used in what are generally categorized as 'frame drums'. In South-East Asia, these are usually drums with a single skin stretched over a frame, but the category also includes double-headed drums. Often the frame is very shallow, and, although deeper frames are also found, their depth is less than the diameter of the skin. A familiar example of a frame drum in the West is the tambourine. The *rammanā*, played in Thailand and Kampuchea (Colour Plate 18 and Plate 4), is similar except that it lacks jingles–though even these are sometimes found attached to frame drums elsewhere in the region. A less shallow frame drum, the single-headed *terbang* used in several sizes in West Java, was graphically compared by Kunst (1973: 216–17) to an old-fashioned wash-basin without a bottom but with a skin stretched across the top. In Peninsular Malaysia and Sumatra, the term *rebana* is used for several types of drum, including frame drums. Possibly the best-known examples of the latter are now the brightly painted *rebana ubi*, played in great numbers by competing village teams in the annual drum festival (*Pesta Rebana Ubi*) which has been promoted as a tourist attraction in Kota Bharu (Colour Plate 11). Although smaller *rebana* are also made, the *rebana ubi* itself is a large and heavy drum which can measure over 90 cm in diameter and weigh up to 110 kg. Its frame is made of hardwood and it has a single, buffalo-hide skin, fitted with rattan bindings. At the base (which is open), about fifteen tuning wedges radiate outwards like spokes from the hub of a wheel.

The most elaborate drumming instrument has been left to last: the Burmese *pat-waìng* or *hsaìng-waìng*. It is, in fact, a one-man drum-chime: a collection of as many as twenty-one tuned drums hung around the inside of a circular wooden frame which is about a metre high and often elaborately decorated (Plate 16). The drums themselves have two laced heads, but are arranged vertically; thus the performer, who sits in the middle of the circle, plays on the upper heads only. With its range of notes covering more than three octaves, the instrument has a melodic function, not merely the usual rhythmic one. Since similar instruments were known in ancient India, it may well be that the *pat-waìng* is a survivor from the early period of Indian influence in South-East Asia.

16. Burmese *pat-waìng*. (By courtesy of the Trustees of the Victoria and Albert Museum, London.)

5

Wind and String Instruments

Flutes

AMONG the musicians whose images were carved at Borobudur were many playing the flute, 'with head to the music bent' and the instrument held sideways (Colour Plate 14). A thousand years later, the posture is still completely familiar: it could have been modelled by any Western flautist today. And, clearly, the ancient instruments did not differ in essentials from modern concert flutes, in spite of the latter's refinements.

Curiously enough, such 'transverse' flutes have disappeared from the traditional music of Central and East Java, and from that of Bali. The majority of South–East Asian flutes are now end-blown (i.e. played with the instrument projecting forwards), but with some variation in the way the sound is generated. The largest single category is represented by the instruments generally called *suling* or *seruling* throughout Indonesia, as well as in Malaysia and the Philippines, but the word is a generic term and in some districts, transverse flutes, too, are known as *suling*.

Ordinarily, the *suling* is a bamboo tube, closed with a node at the top, and open at the bottom. A nick is cut into the node, leading to a small hole in the wall of the instrument. The incision is partly covered by a narrow ring of bamboo or rattan so that the breath is focused into the slit between it and the nick towards the lower edge of the hole. *Suling* are tuned according to the scales employed, and often named after them, e.g. *suling slendro*. Normally they have four, five, or six finger-holes, but there is a good deal of variation in size, ranging from instruments smaller than Western flutes to the long *suling gambuh* of Bali, played with the end resting on the floor.

49

A rather more elaborate instrument is the Thai *khlui* (Colour Plate 18 and Plate 4), together with its equivalents in neighbouring countries. Usually the *khlui*, too, is made of bamboo (though occasionally of ivory or hardwood), but it has a separate mouthpiece and a method of sound production similar to that of the Western recorder. Its most distinctive feature, however, is the buzzing quality of its tone. This is caused by an extra hole, cut in the right-hand side of the instrument and covered by a thin membrane, formerly made of bamboo fibre but now usually of tissue paper. The *khlui* is made in three sizes, each with seven finger-holes (except the smallest, which has six) and a thumb-hole at the back.

Nose flutes, though perhaps more associated with Polynesia and Micronesia, are quite widely used in insular regions of South-East Asia, especially in the northern Philippines, but also in parts of Sabah and Sarawak (Colour Plate 10), and in the Indonesian island of Nias. Most frequently they are held sideways, but some are end-blown. Often they are used in magic and religious rituals, breath emanating from the nose being regarded as having a particular spiritual power.

Reeds

There are two principal types of reed instruments in South-East Asia: oboes and mouth-organs. The oboes are so classified because, like the Western oboe, they have a composite reed, not a single reed as in the clarinet. Nevertheless, these reeds differ in construction from the reeds of Western instruments, and the use of the term 'oboe' can give a misleading impression of the sound-quality they produce. Certainly their timbre has often caused consternation to Europeans. In the middle of the nineteenth century, F. A. Neale, for example, wrote:

The tones produced by this Siamese hautboy, even at the best of time [*sic*], and whilst executing the liveliest airs, are heart-renderingly dolorous and out of tune; nothing will bear comparison with it, with the exception, perhaps, of old and cracked bagpipes, such as the Frenchmen supposed had occasioned the death of all the nightingales in Scotland. (Neale, 1852: 235.)

The Thai name for Neale's 'Siamese hautboy' is *pī*. This, however, is another generic term, and several different types exist. Unless otherwise qualified, *pī* can be taken to mean the commonest form, the *pī nai* (Plates 3 and 24), which consists of a tube (normally made of hardwood but occasionally of marble) about 42 cm long, flared a little at the ends, and with a slight bulge in the middle. There are six finger-holes. Its reed consists of four small pieces of palm leaf tied in two double layers around a short metal tube. The reed itself is taken inside the player's mouth, and the other end of the metal tube is inserted through a disc which closes the near end of the body of the instrument.

Other Thai oboes include the smaller *pī nǫk*, and one with a detachable bell, shaped rather like that of the Western clarinet, the *pī chawā*. Oboes in Kampuchea and Laos are also called *pī*. The Burmese equivalent, the *hnè*, has an optional bell made of metal; if it is used, it is loosely attached and hangs at an angle.

Its name suggests that the *pī chawā* was introduced into Thailand from Java, but, even if that was the case, it was unlikely to have originated there. Oboe-type instruments came from the Middle East, either directly or via India, with the spread of Muslim culture. The folk oboe known in classical Arabic as *surna* became the *serunai* (or *serune*) of Sumatra and Malaysia (Colour Plate 6). In China, it became the *suerna* (or *suona* or *sona*). As far afield as Vietnam, the Cham people play an oboe called *sarunai* or *sarinai*. Instruments of the same basic type go by other names elsewhere, e.g. *selompret* in Central and East Java and in Madura, *pereret* in Bali, and—confusingly—as *tarompet* in Sundanese areas of West Java. Their tense, insistent quality is widely exploited in a number of theatrical genres, and as an accompaniment for fights and for dances which are often of a frenzied nature, notably Javanese hobby-horse dancing (*kuda lumping* or *kuda kepang*).

The mouth-organs are quite different from the Western harmonica. In essentials, they consist of a collection of bamboo pipes, each containing a reed, set in a small wind chest into which air is blown. Instruments meeting this broad description have been known since the second millennium BC in China, where they probably originated and whence they spread to Korea and Japan. In China, they are now called *sheng*, in Korea *saenghwang*, and in Japan *shō*.

In South-East Asia, the most sophisticated version is the *khāēn*, played in Laos and in the north-east of Thailand. The pipes are arranged in a double row and graduated from longest to shortest (Colour Plate 16). Instruments of four different sizes are used, tuned to a scale which—coincidentally—resembles Western diatonic tuning. Their names indicate the numbers of their pipes, the commonest being the *khāēn paet*, typically about a metre in length, with sixteen pipes. The 'reed' in each pipe is in fact a thin tongue of silver or copper, and the admission of air causing it to vibrate is controlled by a finger-hole set a little above the wind chest. Notes can be played in combination as well as singly, and in the hands of a good performer, the *khāēn* is characterized by rapid, virtuoso playing of a very high order.

Other types of mouth-organ are used elsewhere in South-East Asia, mainly amongst tribal groups in its northern parts, but also in Sabah and Sarawak. Both the *sumpotan* (or *sompotan*) in Sabah and the *engkerurai* played by the Iban of Sarawak are simpler instruments than the *khāēn*: their reeds are cut directly from the bamboo pipes, and the pipes are set into the empty shell of a gourd whose stem serves as a blowing pipe (Colour Plate 6).

Trumpets

The distinguishing characteristic of instruments classified as trumpets is that their sounds are produced by lip vibrations. Such instruments are rare in South-East Asia; and with the possible exception of instruments made from or modelled after animal horns, any whose appearance resembles that of Western trumpets of any period are generally relatively recent importations. The long, straight, silver trumpets used in the *nobat* ensembles of the Malaysian courts, for example, came from the Middle East with the establishment of Islam (Colour Plate 4). Western brass instruments arrived later with European travellers and military personnel; but although adopted here and there for ceremonial functions, they had little impact upon indigenous musical traditions.

Some other types of trumpet have a much longer history in the region. Conch-shell trumpets, formed by making a hole in the side or (more usually in South-East Asia) at the apex of a conch, provide what may well be the oldest examples. If, as seems unlikely, they were not already being used, there can be little doubt that they were introduced by the earliest Indian missionaries, for they were important in temple rituals, both Hindu and Buddhist; moreover, they were tokens of royalty and aristocratic caste. Echoes of these ancient associations have persisted into modern times in Thailand, Kampuchea, Burma, and Laos, where shell trumpets are still occasionally used to dignify great ceremonial occasions. As instruments for regular use, however, they are now uncommon except in a few districts, e.g. in the southern Philippines, where they have a signalling rather than a musical function.

Trumpet-type instruments are also made from bamboo. An unusual example, played—usually in groups—in Sabah and Sarawak, is the *kata batang*, which consists of two parallel tubes, one longer and thicker than the other, connected by two short tubes at right angles, with the upper one projecting through the large tube to form a mouthpiece (Colour Plate 15).

Another unusual wind instrument (which may as appropriately be mentioned here as anywhere since, although it is not a trumpet, neither is it a flute nor a reed instrument) is used in imitation of the deepest gongs of the gamelan: in Central Java it is called a *gong bumbung* or *gumbang*, but it has several other names elsewhere in Indonesia. The player sings a low-pitched note, at the same time blowing into an open bamboo tube which is placed inside a much larger tube, closed at one end.

*   *   *

String instruments are much less dominant in South-East Asian than in Western music. They may be divided into three categories: zithers, lutes, and harps. Virtually unknown in the region are the lyre-type instruments familiar in ancient Greece and still common in Africa.

Zithers

In their basic principles, zithers are the simplest of the three categories. They are instruments formed by a string or strings running parallel above the entire length of some kind of support system, usually a wooden board or box. Often the support also acts as a resonator, but this is not essential, and sometimes a separate resonating device is attached.

A rudimentary example came originally from India: it was illustrated in profusion at Borobudur, and although it has not survived in Java, it is still extant in Thailand (*phīn nam tao*) and Kampuchea. It consists of a wooden shaft, slightly bent forward at the bottom to hold a single string. At the top end, the string is connected to a tuning peg which projects through the shaft from behind. Below the peg, a half of a hollowed gourd forms a resonator, attached by its stem to the back of the shaft. In performance, the gourd is pressed against the bare chest of the player, which acts as a further resonating cavity when the string is plucked. In northern Thailand, similar instruments with two or four strings are also used.

Another elementary type of zither consists of a length of bamboo tubing with a thin, longitudinal strip cut (but not detached) from its surface. Two bridges are inserted below this 'string' to enable it to be plucked or lightly struck, and underneath it, an opening is made in the wall of the tube. An example is the Balinese *guntang*, used in ensembles accompanying the popular theatrical form *arja*. Others, sometimes with two or more strings, are found in parts of Java (used to perform the functions of *bonang*, *kenong*, *kempul*, and other similar instruments in rural gamelan ensembles formed entirely of bamboo instruments) and elsewhere, especially in the Philippines (Plate 17).

In many zithers of the region, the strings are supported on a box-type resonator. The Thai *čhakhē*, which can be traced back to at least the fourteenth century, used to be carved to resemble a crocodile, from which it takes its name (Plate 4). Three strings are supported by a bridge at each end and attached to tuning pegs inside the 'tail' end. The strings run over a series of eleven frets, against which they can be pressed with the left hand to control the pitch, and are plucked or strummed with a plectrum held in the right hand. Variants of the instrument are found in Kampuchea (the *tākhe*) and in Burma (the *mí-gyaùng*–see Plate 18). Another type of box zither found in northern parts of the region is trapeziform, with the longest sides parallel and the strings stretched between them, connected to tuning pegs on the shorter sides. It is played with a pair of sticks. The *khim* of Kampuchea, Thailand, and Laos is such an instrument, with fourteen notes, each produced by three strings tuned in unison. Similar instruments are found in

17. Philippine *kulibit* (tube zither).

18. Burmese *mí-gyaùng* (zither): engraving from Yule, 1858: 15.

Burma and Vietnam. All are derived from the Chinese *yangqin*, which in turn was an adaptation of the Persian *sanṭūr* introduced to coastal areas of southern China four or five centuries ago.

A boat-shaped box provides the resonator for the *kacapi*, the plucked zither played in Sundanese areas of West Java, where it makes a popular combination with the *suling*. Two sizes are used: the *kacapi indung* ('mother zither'), which usually has eighteen strings, and the smaller *kacapi anak* ('child zither'). Each string is fixed at one end, and passes over a small, wooden pyramid to a tuning peg fixed into the box. The pyramids can be moved individually for fine tuning (Plate 19). In Central

19. Sundanese *kacapi* (zither).

Java the favoured zither is the *celempung*, whose shallow sound-box, shaped rather like a slightly opened fan, is supported on four legs, the two at the 'open' end being a little longer than the pair at the 'closed' end at which the player sits. Thus the instrument is tilted upwards as he faces it. There are thirteen or fourteen pairs of strings tuned in unison, stretched over a bridge to a series of tuning keys fixed in a transverse wooden bar (Plate 20 and Colour Plate 22). A large gamelan may include three *celempung* tuned like the three *gambang kayu* (see p. 41). In addition, or as a substitute, a higher-pitched and much smaller zither, the *siter*, is sometimes used. Both the *celempung* and the *siter* are plucked, with or without the use of plectra.

20. Javanese *celempung* (zither).

The Vietnamese *dan tranh* is evidence of that country's connections with China. Its ancestry, however, is far more ancient, for it is one of a family of 'long' zithers (including the Japanese *koto* and the Korean *kayagŭm*) related to the indigenous Chinese *zheng* and *qin*, whose history can be traced back for more than two millennia. The *dan tranh* itself consists of a narrow board with one of its sides narrowing a little and a convex resonator on its upper surface, along which run sixteen strings, each supported by a movable bridge (Colour Plate 17). Plectra on fingers of the player's right hand are used to pluck the strings (to the right of the bridges), while the left hand is used to apply pressure to them (on the other side of the bridges) to alter their tension and thus the pitch of the notes. The *dan tranh* is widely played, both as a solo instrument and in ensembles. Another popular Vietnamese zither is the *dan baû*, a long box zither with a single string, struck by a bamboo stick.

Lutes

'Lute' is a generic term, embracing not only the plucked instrument called a lute in the West but also many others, both plucked and bowed. (Bowed types are often described as 'fiddles'.) In this category, indeed, are included not only all the bowed instruments forming the string section of the Western orchestra but also the earlier viols, together with numerous plucked instruments, such as the guitar, mandolin, and banjo. South-East Asia has many examples. Most originated either in China or in the Middle East, though following its introduction by the Portuguese in the seventeenth century, the Western violin can also claim to have been naturalized—both because it is used for the performance of indigenous and not just Western music, and because it is often locally made. In Indonesia and Malaysia, it is known as the *biola* and is generally tuned like the viola.

The Chinese connections are most numerous and striking in Vietnam, but also unmistakable in other northern parts of the region. Several instruments, for example, are clearly akin to the Chinese *erhu*–a long-necked, two-string fiddle with a small sound-box at the lower end covered by snake skin, and an attached bow so arranged that the strings pass between its hair and its stick. They include the Vietnamese *dan nhi* (Colour Plate 19) and the Thai *sǭ duang* (Plate 4) whose sound-boxes are usually made from hardwood. Like the *erhu*, they have no finger-board. Similar instruments but with a sound-box made from a coconut shell are the *dan gao* (Vietnam), *sǭ ū* (Thailand– Plate 4) and *dra û* (Kampuchea). Three very characteristic plucked lutes from China also have Vietnamese relations: the 'moon lute', *yueqin*, whose name is suggested by its large circular sound-box, is close to the Vietnamese *dan doan* ('Chinese lute'); the long-necked *sanxian* to the *dan tam*; and the pear-shaped *pipa* to the *dan ty ba*.

The principal areas of Middle Eastern influence are Indonesia and Malaysia. There, the most common string instrument is a fiddle played with a separate bow, whose origins are implied by its name, *rebab* (a variant of the Arabic *rabab*)*, and which can be assumed to be a legacy from the spread of Islam. The Central Javanese version is a two-string instrument with a roughly heart-shaped sound-box covered by a thin skin of material such as buffalo intestine at the bottom of a long neck. It has a spike at its base, rather like a cello, and is played in an upright position (Plate 21). Again, there is no finger-board: the strings are merely pressed lightly, without touching the neck. The tone, though lacking the resonance and potential for virtuosity of the violin, has considerable lyrical expressiveness, and the single *rebab* player in the modern gamelan has an important role as leader in melodic aspects of the music. In Sumatra and other parts of Indonesia, as well as in Malaysia, the *rebab* exists in slightly different forms. The most important

21. Javanese *rebab* on stand.

22. *Tarawangsa*: fiddle from West Java.

version in Peninsular Malaysia, for example, is a three-string instrument (*rebab tiga tali*–Colour Plate 6). Thailand has a similar fiddle with three strings, the *sǭ sām sāi* (Colour Plate 18 and Plate 4).

Another instrument popular in many Muslim districts is the *gambus*, a plucked lute with a short neck and a large, pear-shaped body resembling the Middle Eastern *'ūd*. It usually has seven to twelve strings, most tuned in unison pairs, and is played as a solo instrument, or to accompany a singer, or in groups–notably the *orkes gambus* (*gambus* orchestra). Some other types of lute are more localized, and more probably indigenous: they include the bowed *tarawangsa* (now quite rare) in West Java (Plate 22) and the plucked *sapeh* or *sapih* in Sarawak (Colour Plate 6). In Thailand, the *krajappī* (Colour Plate 18) is a plucked lute made in various sizes, but always characterized by a large, oval resonating-box and a long, fretted neck supporting two double courses of strings, played with a plectrum. It has a venerable history as an ensemble instrument, and although it fell out of favour towards the end of the nineteenth century, it has since made something of a come-back in modernized forms.

Harps

Except in Burma, harps are now almost unknown in South-East Asia, though they must once have been familiar–there are many representations at Borobudur, Angkor, and elsewhere. In Burma, however, the ancient *saùng-gauk* is still prominent and highly regarded. The earliest representation of it in the country itself dates from the seventh century AD, but it appears to have been brought (together with its associations as a court instrument) from India, whence it may have arrived much earlier from Mesopotamia, where similar instruments existed in the third millennium BC.

It has a wooden, boat-shaped resonator, the upper surface of which is covered with deerskin, and a tall arch rising from the prow, curving inwards. The strings (sixteen in modern instruments) run diagonally from the resonator to the arch, to which they are fastened by tasselled tuning cords (Colour Plate 20). In performance, the instrument is held in the player's lap, with the arch to the left. The right hand is used to pluck the strings, while the left hand may adjust their pitch by pressing on them near the arch. Traditionally used as an accompaniment for court songs, the *saùng-gauk* began also to be used as a virtuoso instrument in the eighteenth century, a tradition maintained and developed by many contemporary performers of outstanding skill and artistry.

6

Ensembles

WHILE some of the instruments in the preceding chapters can be played alone, scarcely any are exclusively used solo, and most are viable only in an ensemble. South-East Asian music, in fact, is very largely ensemble music. To the outside world, the best-known ensembles are undoubtedly the large gamelan orchestras of Java and Bali, though it must be said at once that this perception represents a somewhat distorted perspective. Apart from the fact that there are many other ensembles in Indonesia—all known as various types of 'gamelan'—there are also many other categories elsewhere in the region. Nevertheless, since the large gamelans do in many respects represent the furthest development of widespread principles, they may justifiably take pride of place in any survey of instrumental ensembles in South-East Asia.

To Indonesians, 'gamelan' denotes a particular set of instruments—the actual instruments, not the performers or the music they play. Different terms are used for what in English it is convenient to describe as 'gamelan music', 'gamelan players', 'gamelan orchestras', and 'gamelan concerts'. The word itself is used primarily in Java and Bali, but has been retained elsewhere (e.g. in parts of Malaysia) to refer to sets of instruments transported by Javanese and Balinese immigrants.

Although many individual gamelan instruments have existed in all essentials for a thousand years or more, the history of their organization into the modern ensembles is shadowy. As far as Central Java is concerned, it is generally agreed that they first formed separate groups of loud and soft instruments for outdoor and indoor use respectively (indeed, such ensembles are still used), and that about the seventeenth century, the two groups were combined to form the precursor of the modern, large gamelan. Early gamelans consisted of either *slendro* or *pelog* instruments, not both. Such single tuning–system gamelans (*gamelan sepangkon*) are still common, but in the nineteenth century a new practice developed of combining two gamelans, one in *slendro* and one in *pelog*, to form a 'double' gamelan (*gamelan seprangkat*–Colour Plates 22 and 23). The two sets of instruments are never played simultaneously, though they are generally tuned with one note in common. Their combination in one ensemble makes it possible for pieces in either tuning to be performed, and with quick changes between the two.

The following table shows a typical constitution of a large (but not exceptional) *gamelan seprangkat* in Surakarta, Central Java. One in nearby Yogyakarta would be almost the same except in a few details–for example, it might also include a lower version of the *bonang*, the *bonang panembung*, in both tunings.

	Instruments		*Performers*
Gong ageng	1 or 2		
Gong suwuk/			1 or 2
siyem	3		
Kempul	4 in *slendro*;	5 in *pelog*	
Kenong	5 in *slendro*;	6–7 in *pelog*	1
Ketuk	1 in *slendro*;	1 in *pelog*	
Kempyang	1 in *slendro*;	1 in *pelog*	1
Kendang			
gending	1		
Kendang kalih	1		1
Kendang ciblon	1		
Rebab	1 in *slendro*;	1 in *pelog*	1
Saron panerus	2 in *slendro*;	2 in *pelog*	2
Saron barung	4 in *slendro*;	4 in *pelog*	4
Saron demung	2 in *slendro*;	2 in *pelog*	2

	Instruments		Performers
Slentem	1 in *slendro*;	1 in *pelog*	1
Bonang panerus	1 in *slendro*;	1 in *pelog*	1
Bonang barung	1 in *slendro*;	1 in *pelog*	1
Gender panerus	1 in *slendro*;	2 in *pelog*	1
Gender barung	1 in *slendro*;	2 in *pelog*	1
Gambang kayu	1 in *slendro*;	2 in *pelog*	1
Suling	1 in *slendro*;	1 in *pelog*	1
Celempung (or *Siter*)	1 in *slendro*;	2 in *pelog*	1

Singers:

> *Pesinden* (female soloists) 1–8
> *Gerongan* (male chorus) 0–8

In the eastern and western parts of Java, large ensembles roughly equivalent to those of the central region are also found, but in addition, both areas have distinctive types of gamelan of their own. Amongst the most characteristic is the *gamelan degung* (tuned to a five-note *pelog* scale) of the Sundanese people in the west. Originally a small, refined court ensemble which was never completely standardized, the *gamelan degung* has tended to expand in recent years. Earlier, it included only a few instruments: a set of medium-pitched bossed gongs (*jengglong*), either suspended from a rack or lying on crossed cords in a frame; a *bonang* (see p. 28); a *saron*; a large gong; a short end-blown flute (*suling degung*); and a pair of drums (*kendang*)—and not invariably all of these. Later optional additions included further instruments of the *saron* type, a xylophone (*gambang kayu*), a *rebab* instead of the *suling*, and also voices.

Balinese gamelan shares a common stock with that of Java, but the two traditions began to branch in different directions in the sixteenth century. The incoming tide of Islam never reached Bali, and many Javanese nobles who did not embrace the new faith moved there with their courts. From that time until the early years of the twentieth century, the feudal society of Bali remained very largely cut off from the political, religious, and cultural forces at work in Java itself, and its musical traditions consequently developed independently.

There is a broad family resemblance between Balinese and Javanese gamelan instruments—a few indeed are identical, and most are similar in essentials—but they are sometimes used differently and rarely share the same names. An immediately distinctive feature is that, in Bali, keyed instruments are played in pairs with one tuned fractionally sharper than the other, producing a very characteristic vibrato effect. What is most remarkable about Balinese gamelan, however, is its astonishing development during the twentieth century. It is true that Javanese gamelan, too, has evolved, but whereas there the emphasis has been on elaboration and expansion (e.g. increasing numbers of *kempul* and *kenong*), in Bali there occurred a veritable explosion of musical creativity which led to a re-ordering of the gamelan as an ensemble and to changes in individual instruments.

The Balinese equivalents of the Javanese gamelan described earlier are known as *gamelan gong* or, more commonly, simply as *gong*, to which other words are added to indicate particular types of ensemble. The largest version, the 'great' *gong–gamelan gong gede* (or *gong gede*)—has been largely superseded, but at the beginning of the twentieth century it was a dignified ceremonial ensemble which could include some forty instruments, tuned to a kind of five-note *pelog* scale called *selisir*. Roughly half were five-note instruments of the *saron* and *gender* types, concerned with presenting the *pokok*, i.e. basic melody. (Single-octave members of the *saron* and *gender* families are generally referred to collectively as *gangsa* (bronze), although the word is sometimes restricted to one category or the other. *Gangsa gantung* refers specifically to *gender* types (*gantung* = suspended) (Plate 23), and *gangsa jongkok* to instruments with keys resting

23. Balinese *gangsa gantung*.

(*jongkok* = squatting) on the wooden resonator, such as the *saron*.) In the *gamelan gong gede*, the *gender* types are used in groups at three different octave-levels. From highest to lowest, they are called *penyacah*, *jublag*, and *jegogan*. The *jegogan* merely outline the *pokok* by picking out notes at regular intervals.

Except for the *jegogan*, which are struck with a padded stick, they are played with a murderous-looking mallet with a head of wood or horn, resulting in a bright, penetrating sound utterly unlike the gentle murmuring of Javanese *gender*. The player holds the mallet in the right hand, using the left to damp the notes, as in *saron* playing. Other instruments in the *gong gede* include the *trompong pengarap* and *gede*, a four-gong *reyong*, and several pairs of *ceng-ceng* (cymbals). Fewer suspended gongs are used than in Central Java, but like the drums (*kendang*), they are similar.

The new style of musical composition which began to emerge early in the century and was to change the face of Balinese music was known as *kebyar*. It is characterized by the exciting effect of its explosive outbursts of sound, its tense syncopations, brilliant sonorities, and virtuosic display. *Kebyar* music rapidly achieved an almost feverish popularity and is now the type of music for which the island is perhaps best known. It led to considerable modifications in the *gamelan gong*, and ultimately to a new form, the *gamelan gong kebyar* or *gong kebyar*, though smaller versions of the earlier *gamelan gong* may still be heard in the villages, used for ceremonial purposes. The *saron* disappeared, the *trompong* was abandoned (unless required for old ceremonial music), the modern *reyong* (with its range of two and a half octaves) was substituted for the earlier type, and fewer cymbals–lighter and smaller–were used (see McPhee, 1976: 328). The highest *gangsa gantung* were replaced by groups of two new, ten-key versions (one at the higher octave), which were employed in elaborate ornamentation, often demanding great virtuosity (Colour Plate 21). *Gangsa* keys are not, in fact, always suspended: though this method is preferred in southern Bali because of the richer sonority it produces, in the North the keys are supported above their resonators on cushions of felt, cork or some similar substance, like those of *saron*, resulting in a more brilliant quality. Javanese gamelan instruments not normally found in the *gong kebyar* include the *rebab*, the *gambang kayu*, and the *celempung*; but at least one flute (*suling*) is to be expected, and often two. *Gong kebyar* ensembles are not restricted to music composed specially for them; they may also play items from the repertory of the old *gamelan gong* or other types of gamelan, though for this purpose additional instruments and some modifications in their constitution may be needed.

Elsewhere in South-East Asia, there are also ensembles consisting primarily of gongs, gong-chimes, and drums. The Thai equivalent of the gamelan, for example, the *pī phāt*, includes at least one circular rack of gong-kettles (*khọ̄ng wong yai*), a xylophone (*ranāt ēk*), drums (a *taphōn* and two *klọ̄ng that*), a pair of tiny cymbals (*ching*), and a *pī*, the oboe-type instrument after which it is named (Plates 3 and 24). Larger versions of the same ensemble may add a second oboe, a differently sized gong-chime and xylophone (*khọ̄ng wong lek* and *ranāt thum*), larger cymbals (*chāp lek* and possibly *chāp yai*), a suspended gong (*khọ̄ng mōng*), the metal-keyed 'xylophones' (*ranāt ēk lek* and *ranāt thum lek*), and possibly other instruments as well. In Kampuchea, the *pinpeat* (or *biṇ bādy*) closely resembles the Thai *pī phāt*. Similar, too, is the Burmese *hsaìng-waìng*, though this always includes the very distinctive circle of tuned drums from which it takes its name (see p. 48).

Another Thai ensemble, the *mahōrī*, was originally a group of two string instruments, a drum, and a singer who also kept time with clappers. It is now larger and more varied, though retaining an emphasis on string instruments. Even the smallest version usually includes one each of the strings, *sọ̄ sām sāi*, *sọ̄ duang*, *sọ̄ ū*, and *čhakhē*, together with a flute (*khlui*), xylophone (*ranāt ēk*), gong-chime (*khọ̄ng wong*), cymbals (*ching*), and drums (*thōn* and *rammanā*). In larger *mahōrī*, the strings may be doubled, with the addition of another flute and further percussion instruments (Plate 4).

24. Thai *pī phāt* ensemble: illustration from a book (*c.*1730) which
survived the destruction of the then Thai capital, Ayutthaya, in
1767 [printed as frontispiece in Morton, 1979]. Instruments at the
bottom of the picture include, from left to right: front row—*pī
nai* (oboe), *taphōn* (drum), *khǫng wong* (gong-circle); back
row—*klǫng that* (drum), *ranāt ēk* (xylophone), and *pōeng māng*
(drum).

Ensembles such as these and the large gamelan mentioned earlier represent the acme of development and polish. They have their roots in the courts, and their natural habitat is still a sophisticated and generally urban one in spite of the fact that the courts themselves have now largely disappeared, or at least have declined in influence. In rural areas, the situation is more diverse. Throughout the region, popular music-making over many centuries has resulted in an endless array of ensembles, covering a wide spectrum of size, complexity, and refinement. Their individual features have been conditioned by many factors: environment, history, economic circumstances, as well as simple local preference. Particularly in the more remote districts, ancient traditions have often remained untouched by the upheavals of the twentieth century, though it is equally true that elsewhere they have been coloured by modern musical fashions, if only to the extent of adopting popular Western instruments.

The majority of South-East Asian ensembles, from the most primitive to the most refined, include instruments of different kinds—gongs, drums, xylophones, strings, and wind, though not necessarily all of these. But there are some which consist of a single category only, or in which a single category is heavily predominant. The bamboo gamelans (*gamelan bumbung*) used in Central and East Java as inexpensive substitutes for the gong-based gamelan, provide an example. Another is to be found in the *kulintang* ensembles of gongs mentioned on pp. 26 and 28. In the Minahassa region of North Sulawesi, characteristic ensembles consisting entirely of xylophones (*kolintang*) are used; while in West Java, large groups of *angklung* (with perhaps twenty or more players, each with two or three instruments) are popular. Some of these *angklung* 'orchestras' have extended their repertoire to include arrangements of such well-worn Western favourites as 'The Blue Danube' and 'Colonel Bogey', by means of instruments tuned to provide the full range of notes in the Western chromatic scale.

25. A nineteenth-century gamelan at Makassar (now Ujung Pandang) in southern Celebes. (Coloured lithograph by C. Ritsema after E. Dubois from *Types Indiens pris au Marché à Sourabaya* (Haarlem, 1860).)

Ensembles consisting exclusively or mainly of strings are uncommon except in northern parts of the region, whose proximity to China has led to a wider and more varied use of strings generally. This is especially striking in Vietnam, where entertainment groups, for example, are frequently formed from combinations of instruments such as the *dan tranh* (zither), *dan nhi* (two-string fiddle), *dan nguyêt* (a long-necked, moon-shaped lute), and *dan ty ba* (pear-shaped lute).

Southern Vietnam has also shown a readiness to adopt Western string instruments, notably the violin and guitar, for use in popular ensembles. This is by no means a new departure in South-East Asia. Reference has already been made (p. 59) to the introduction of the violin in the seventeenth century but an entire ensemble based on Western instruments, the Indonesian *kroncong* (or *keroncong*), can date its history back to about the same period or even slightly earlier. Its origins appear to lie in the music brought to eastern parts of Indonesia (especially the Moluccas) by Portuguese sailors and settlers.

Kroncong is the word used to denote an instrument and a musical genre as well as an ensemble. The instrument is a kind of small guitar handmade in Indonesia and Malaysia. The genre consists of easy-going, sentimental songs using the diatonic scales of Western music, and written in a style whose simple melodic shaping and elementary harmonic progressions are derived from the jargon of Western popular music. The ensemble is traditionally dominated by plucked strings (such as the guitar, mandolin, banjo, ukulele, double-bass, and—very characteristically—the cello played *pizzicato*), with one or more violins (bowed), a transverse flute, and light percussion instruments such as bongo drums and tambourine. More recently, the addition of instruments such as the vibraphone, electric guitar, electronic organ, and synthesizer have been one indication of the influence of modern Western rock and pop music. As a musical style, therefore, *kroncong* is certainly something of a hybrid, but it has developed an authentically Indonesian character. Formerly identified particularly with Jakarta, it has become hugely popular in other urban centres throughout the Republic, and indeed beyond, as, for example, in Malaysia. Moreover, it often betrays distinctive musical characteristics of the different localities in which it is performed. The *orkes Melayu* is another ensemble which uses Western instruments (though not exclusively) and plays harmonized music.

Special Ensembles

Ensembles such as the large gamelan of Central Java and the Thai *pī phāt* are used in a variety of contexts. There are others, however, with a more limited use, most commonly as an accompaniment to various forms of drama and dance. Shadow-puppet plays provide a case in point. In Bali, for example, they are accompanied by a *gamelan wayang* consisting of one or two pairs of ten-key *gender*. Each of Malaysia's three distinct *wayang kulit* traditions (of which the *wayang siam* is the most popular and, in spite of its name, the indigenous form) is also characterized by a small but distinctive ensemble. Even Central Java, which often uses the full *gamelan seprangkat* in *wayang kulit*, retains some special instruments and playing techniques associated with the traditional and smaller type, the *gamelan wayangan*, tuned in *slendro* only.

Bali has a particularly rich inheritance of distinctive ensembles associated with particular types of theatre and dance, such as the *gamelan wayang* mentioned earlier. Many, however, have become rare, e.g. the *gamelan gambuh* (with four long flutes, *suling gambuh*, and a *rebab* as its melodic instruments). The *gamelan pelegongan*, used to accompany the *legong* dance, is a large gamelan including one or two pairs of thirteen-key *gender* which are played like Javanese *gender* with two sticks, though with wooden heads; but in common with other such ensembles, it has tended to go out of fashion and to be replaced by the *gamelan gong*.

As mentioned in Chapter 2, many kinds of dance and drama throughout South-East Asia have a spiritual dimension, yet there is little music which is exclusively associated with formal religious rituals, certainly within the temples or mosques themselves, and nothing to compare with the vast corpus of liturgical music in the West. In a more nearly domestic context, however, religious rites of passages are not infrequently carried out to the sound of ensembles peculiar to them. Funeral ceremonies and death rites provide the most common examples, such as the Balinese *gamelan angklung* (named after the bamboo rattles, though it now rarely includes them) and the *gamelan gambang*, consisting of a quartet of large xylophones and one or two *saron*. Individual sets of instruments of this kind are sometimes venerated as sacred objects, not used or brought into public view except on appropriate occasions.

Something of the same awe attaches to the *nobat* ensembles belonging to certain Peninsular Malaysian courts (Colour Plate 4). They were introduced into the region from the Middle East not later than the early fifteenth century as marks of sovereignty. Indeed, they seem to have supplanted the earlier use of a crown, although this has been revived in the nineteenth century. The detailed composition of the ensembles varies, but the oldest, the one in Kedah, is reasonably typical in consisting of a metal kettledrum (*negara* or *nengkara*) and a long silver trumpet (*nafiri*)–both, of course, highly unusual in the region–plus two double-headed drums (*gendang*), an oboe (*serunai*), and a suspended gong. Its players form a hereditary élite.

Ensembles such as these are by their very nature usually of considerable antiquity, often embodying musical traditions older even than the most venerable instruments still extant. Examples are to be found in ancient types of gamelan which

26. *Gamelan sekati* at the senior conservatory for traditional music (ASKI) in Surakarta, Central Java.

to this day maintain particular religious and ceremonial functions in the Javanese courts: the *gamelan munggang*, *gamelan koḍok ngorek*, *gamelan carabalen*, and *gamelan sekati* or *sekaten*. The first three have distinctive tunings: *munggang*, a three-note quasi-*pelog* scale; *koḍok ngorek*, a three-note quasi-*slendro* scale; and *carabalen*, a four- to six-note form of *pelog*. Their limited pitch resources alone might imply a primitive origin, and although this is fertile ground for the imaginative, the claim that at least in essentials they can be dated back to the third or fourth century AD is not impossible. By such standards, the *gamelan sekati* (tuned to a more conventional seven-note *pelog*, but pitched exceptionally low) must be accounted a newcomer: it was probably devised around the beginning of the sixteenth century.

All four of these gamelan types are highly idiosyncratic in their instrumental resources and make use of instruments not commonly employed elsewhere. The *gamelan sekati*, for example, includes an unusually large drum (*beḍug*) as well as exceptionally big *saron* and *bonang* kettles, but none of the soft instruments (Plate 26). It is played each year, in a stunningly loud and forceful style, to celebrate the birthday of the Prophet Muhammad.

Bibliography

Sources Quoted or Mentioned

Crawfurd, J., *History of the Indian Archipelago*, Vol. 1 (London, 1820).

Frame, Edward M., 'The Musical Instruments of Sabah, Malaysia', *Ethnomusicology*, XXVI/2 (May 1982).

Kunst, J., *Music in Java*, 2 vols. (The Hague, Martinus Nijhoff, 1949 [originally published in Dutch in 1934]; 3rd ed. rev. E. L. Heins, 1973).

McPhee, C., *Music in Bali* (New Haven and London, Yale University Press, 1966; reprint New York, Da Capo Press, 1976).

Morton, D., *The Traditional Music of Thailand* (Berkeley, University of California Press, 1979).

Neale, F. A., *Narrative of a Residence at the Capital of the Kingdom of Siam* (London, 1852).

Raffles, T. S., *The History of Java*, Vol. 1 (London, 1817; reprint Singapore, Oxford University Press, 1988).

Yule, Henry, *A Narrative of the Mission to the Court of Ava in 1855* (London, 1858; reprint Kuala Lumpur, Oxford University Press, 1968).

Finding Out More

The basic work of reference is *The New Grove Dictionary of Musical Instruments* (3 vols., London, Macmillan, 1984). There are also valuable entries under the various countries of the region in *The New Grove Dictionary of Music and Musicians* (20 vols., London, Macmillan, 1980). Both of these contain far more extensive bibliographies than would be feasible here, but mention may be made of a few works which may be particularly helpful to people beginning to explore the subject. *Music Cultures of the Near Pacific, the Near East and Asia* by William P. Malm (2nd ed., New Jersey, Prentice Hall, 1977) includes a useful survey of South-East Asian music, and puts it in a wider context. Three weighty regional studies are: Jaap Kunst's *Music in Java*, Colin McPhee's *Music in Bali*, and David Morton's *The Traditional Music of Thailand*. Jennifer Lindsay's *Javanese Gamelan* (Kuala Lumpur, Oxford University Press, 1979) provides an informative introductory account, and Colin McPhee's autobiographical *A House in Bali* (London, Gollancz, 1947; paperback reprint Kuala Lumpur, Oxford University Press, 1979) should not be missed—not least because it is such a good read. *Theatre in Southeast Asia* by James R. Brandon (Cambridge, Massachusetts, Harvard University Press, 1967) is a work of thorough scholarship which pays due attention to the importance of music in the region's dramatic forms.

Gramophone recordings are much more difficult to pin-point. Locally made cassette tapes (usually very cheap, if erratic in quality) are abundant in many areas, but can rarely be obtained outside their immediate locality. Any information they may give is unlikely to be in English. Western commercial recordings (mostly on disc) are often excellent and well annotated, but they do not always remain very long in the catalogue and so it is essential to consult up-to-date lists. Among the more established labels may be mentioned Archiv, Bärenreiter (Musicaphon), EMI Italiana (Musical Atlas–Unesco Collection), Le Chant du Monde, Lyrichord, Nonesuch, Ocora, Philips (Unesco Collection–Musical Sources), Playasound, and Tangent. Reviews of new recordings and publications appear in two relevant scholarly journals: *Asian Music* (Society for Asian Music, Department of Asian Studies, Cornell University, New York 14853, USA) and *Ethnomusicology* (Society for Ethnomusicology, P.O. Box 2984, Ann Arbor, Michigan 48106, USA).

Index